Obeah, Christ and Rastaman

Obeah, Christ and Rastaman
Jamaica and its Religion

Ivor Morrish

James Clarke & Co.

The Lutterworth Press

P.O. Box 60
Cambridge
CB1 2NT
United Kingdom

www.lutterworth.com
publishing@lutterworth.com

Paperback ISBN: 978 0 7188 9528 0
PDF ISBN: 978 0 7188 4747 0
ePub ISBN: 978 0 7188 4748 7

British Library Cataloguing in Publication Data
A record is available from the British Library

First published by The Lutterworth Press, 1982
This edition published 2022

Copyright © 1982 Ivor Morrish

All rights reserved. No part of this edition may be reproduced, stored electronically or in any retrieval system, or transmitted in any form or by any means, electronic, mechanical, photocopying, recording, or otherwise, without prior written permission from the Publisher (permissions@lutterworth.com).

To Carl

Contents

Author's Preface		ix
Chapter 1.	Introduction	1
Chapter 2.	The Culture and Religion of the Aborigines	3
Chapter 3.	The Peoples of Jamaica	9
Chapter 4.	The African Origins of Jamaican Slaves	13
Chapter 5.	Some Aspects of African Religion	17
Chapter 6.	Treatment of Slaves in the Caribbean	25
Chapter 7.	Jamaican Slaves and Christianity	32
Chapter 8.	African Survivals	40
Chapter 9.	Revivalism and Pocomania	49
Chapter 10.	Cumina and Other Ceremonies	59
Chapter 11.	The Rastafarians	68
Chapter 12.	Christian Sects and Denominations	92
Chapter 13.	Religion and Jamaican Society	102
Chapter 14.	Conclusion	111
Bibliography		114
Appendices:		
1.	Sects and Denominations	116
2.	West Africa: Some Ethnic Groups	119
3.	Jamaica: Parish boundaries	120
Index		121

Author's Preface

Jamaica has been called 'a museum of religions', but although many hundreds of religious sects and groups are represented in Jamaica it is no more of a 'museum' than almost any other society in this respect. At any rate it is a very lively and living museum which deserves a much closer examination than has so far been afforded it. The present book provides a brief introduction to a very stimulating study – the way in which the Jamaican society has developed religiously, and the manner in which her various cults, sects and denominations react with the total social scene.

This study arose originally out of field research done in Jamaica under the auspices of the Department of Education and Science, and with the aid of grants generously provided by the Joseph Rowntree Charitable Trust, the Joseph Rowntree Social Service Trust, and La Sainte Union College of Higher Education, Southampton. Needless to say, none of these bodies is in any way responsible for any of the opinions expressed in this book.

I would like to thank all those in Jamaica, too numerous to name, who assisted me in my researches and gave me the benefit of their time and experience. I am particularly indebted to Joe Owens S.J. of the Social Action Centre, Kingston for keeping me in touch with various developments in recent years in Jamaica. My special thanks go to Howard Williams H.M.I., a constant and unstinting source of information, to Euan Reid of West Midlands College for tapes and other material, to Jack Zoltie and Denis Ince who proved to be two very lively and helpful companions in our tour of most of the island, and finally to Adrian Brink of James Clarke & Co. for his encouragement.

Ivor Morrish
Caterham
Surrey

Chapter 1
Introduction

There are few countries, of whatever size, which present the individual interested in religion with such a wealth of historical, psychological, sociological and theological material as the island of Jamaica. It is a veritable treasure-house of religious ideas, groups, sects, cults and movements which derive from both the Old World and the New.

Wherever man exists there are concepts of God, religion, powers, spirits, ghosts and magical means of manipulating the physical as well as the spiritual. There are the orthodox, the liberals, the modernists, the black witches, the white magicians, the spiritualists and those who look to some millennium when all man's material and spiritual problems will be resolved; and Jamaica is certainly no exception. Most of the religious and religio-political movements of the world are to be found epitomized in some form in Jamaica. It is a country full of colour, hope, yearning, depression, despair, utopian dreams, nostalgic longings, gaiety, fear, belief, doubt and superstition.

The present approach to the subject is both historical and sociological; and it looks at the religious conditions of a people who have, over the years, suffered incredible degradation and suppression. They were provided with a patent dual morality by an imperial slave-trading society – the Christian ideal beyond their realization and the more easily attainable slave morality – and they have endured the impingement of every kind of sectarian Christian mission.

It might well be possible to classify all the religious cults and movements in Jamaica, as elsewhere, by means of some convenient sociological typology. But to seek to do so would be to lose some of the life and the existential drama of the whole process, as well as to force a somewhat artificial framework upon something that is in a very real sense incommensurable. Such typologies are fictions, however useful, designed to facilitate understanding of social causation and human reaction to deep personal need.

The needs of the Jamaicans, in religious terms, are met in a great variety of ways. There are, nevertheless, certain common denominators in their religious experience. It is interesting to note, for example, the extent to which the rituals of magic and similar patterns of psychic and spiritual behaviour permeate most of their religious sects and cults. There is something elemental about their religious experience which harks back to their African ancestors' beliefs.

In order, therefore, to understand fully the development of the variety of religion in Jamaica it is necessary to have a look at the historical origins and background of the Jamaican people, their treatment by so-called civilized societies, and their own search for an identity through their religious faith and their religio-political movements. Some still persisting practices in Jamaica, such as obeah, are not conducive to the healthy development of their society, and are forbidden by law.

There are many other vestiges of African cults, which have survived through the years of slavery down to modern times. A few have been resuscitated somewhat artificially long after they have died a natural death, in order, according to the indigenous belief, to establish or re-establish a cultural identity and solidarity.

Chapter 2
Culture and Religion of the Aborigines

It might perhaps be argued that any consideration of the culture and religion of an aboriginal people, who had certainly disappeared from Jamaica by 1655 if not much earlier, is irrelevant to any discussion of religion as it exists in Jamaica today; but aboriginal cultures have a habit of persisting, often in a superficially unrecognizable form, as we know only too well from some of the accretions to Christian culture and practice from indigenous rites and beliefs. This chapter may, therefore, be regarded as a lengthy footnote to the history of religion in Jamaica.

The aborigines of Jamaica were Amerindians. There were, in fact, various groups or tribes of Amerindians who migrated into the Central American area, as well as into the Caribbean, from North and South America. The Arawaks, the tribal group with whom we are here particularly concerned, settled in the islands of the Greater Antilles; whilst the Caribs, another Amerindian group, occupied the smaller islands of the Lesser Antilles.

It is probable that the Arawaks discovered another primitive tribe – a people called the Ciboneys or Siboneys – already inhabiting the islands of Cuba and Haiti, if not also Jamaica itself. Although it is not certain precisely where these latter tribes originated, it is now generally believed that they made their way down from North America, probably from the region of Florida. The Ciboneys, whose name means 'dwellers of the rocks', lived in caves along the seashore and spent a large part of their time fishing. It has been suggested that the Arawaks made the Ciboneys their slaves, although evidence for this is unclear.

Both the Arawaks and the Caribs originally lived in the northern area of South America, namely, Venezuela and the Guianas, where descendants of the Arawaks are still to be found. The Arawaks were the first to leave the mainland and they eventually settled in Jamaica, probably at the beginning of the eleventh century. They were undoubtedly very skilled as seamen, using dug-out canoes which might carry over seventy men. Columbus recorded that he saw one such canoe which measured about ninety-six feet in length and eight feet in breadth.

The Arawaks, a peace-loving people, were soon pursued by the Caribs, who were very savage and cruel, and who bade fair to destroy the Arawaks in much the same way as they did the Ciboneys. The

Caribs were cannibalistic; in fact, both the English word cannibal and the Spanish *canibal* are held to be variants of Carib. The Caribs descended upon the islands in their long war-canoes, similar to the canoes of the Arawaks, and meted out death and destruction to the Ciboneys, taking captive their women and torturing and eating their men. Only the arrival of Columbus in the Caribbean area in 1492 called a halt to their ravaging activities, and prevented the Caribs from finally overrunning the islands of the Greater Antilles – Cuba, Haiti and Jamaica.

Carib religion was similar to that of the Arawaks. It was animistic, but it also laid a considerable emphasis upon courage and bravery in war, which obviously helped their religion, particularly in terms of conquest and expansion. The peace-loving Arawaks were easy meat for the Caribs and they were clearly not organised for survival. Indeed, the Caribs envisaged a sort of Amerindian Shangri-La in which the souls of their courageous warriors were ministered to by conquered Arawak slaves. On the other hand, the cowards among the Carib warriors, always an object of utter contempt and scorn in Amerindian history, went to a barren, waste land where they served the effeminate Arawaks. It was the emphasis on prowess in war which made the product of Carib animism so different from that of the Arawaks.

The Arawaks were basically a simple, gentle people who lived in huts shaped like those of the peasants of Jamaica, and they slept in hammocks. Their huts were either circular or rectangular; the round hut had a long central post that helped to support a roof which was cone-shaped and composed of thatched grass and palm leaves. The Arawaks were satisfied with a minimum of effort in life for a minimum return. Certainly they did not make a fetish of hard work; and it was not really their nature to fight, so they put up very little resistance to the continued attacks of the Caribs. They simply wished to live comfortable, peaceable and undisturbed lives.

Whilst the Arawaks were scattered fairly widely over the island of Jamaica, there was a tendency for them to live near the sea or near rivers. The men spent much time fishing and catching turtles whilst their womenfolk grew corn, cassava and sweet potatoes. Fishing was effected by both nets and bone-tipped spears. Cashew-nuts, naseberry plums, star-apples and guava fruit, all of which grew wild on the island, formed part of the staple diet, as did yellow snakes, conies and iguanas, and distilled intoxicating potions from cassava and maize.

The Arawaks were a pleasure-loving people. They wore very few clothes except on festival occasions; and those they did wear – usually small loin-cloths – were made of twisted fibres from cotton growing wild. They smoked a plant called *cohiba*, which they cultivated widely. After some slight preparation they inhaled it through a *tabaco*, or Y-shaped tube, which was inserted in the nose; deep inhalation quickly produced unconsciousness. *Cohiba* was thus used as a form of tranquillizer and probably helped to contribute to the pacific nature of the Arawaks.

An Arawak village might comprise upwards of fifty families, led by a chief, or *cacique*, who had considerable power over the village. The present-day Maroon village of Accompong is ruled almost completely by the 'Colonel', or headman. He is the modern equivalent of the *cacique*; all visitors are immediately referred to him, and he is responsible in an almost despotic manner for the solution of all local disagreements and problems.

In general, monogamy was the rule among the Arawaks; only the *cacique* was permitted to have a number of wives. He was expected to be vigorous and healthy, and if a *cacique* was ill and dying it would be regarded as a mark of special favour to strangle him. Other very sick people would be left to die in the bush.

Much of what has been written concerning Arawak life and beliefs is based upon the information and descriptions provided by Columbus. Apparently they were a short people, although fairly well-proportioned, with straight black hair, copper-coloured skin, and somewhat flat features. The shaping of the head was induced from infancy by tying a board to the forehead, which made it both flat and hard. This was a fairly common practice among the Indians of South America; the Incas in particular used to employ two boards bound tightly to the front and back of the baby's head, before the fontanelle had fully closed over and the parietal bones had firmly knitted. In this way the head became elongated, a sign of beauty.

The religion of the Arawaks was basically animistic; that is, to them all life was informed by some spiritual essence or anima. It was a world of spirits in which all areas of nature were interpenetrated by spiritual power. As with most, if not all, primitive groups, the Arawaks invented stories in order to explain the origins of things, of life and of situations. These aetiological myths seek to give an explanation for the causes of things where no 'scientific' explanation or description is available. All forms of life ultimately emanated from two deities, one male and the other female, who were responsible for the continuing fertility of all forms of nature. Both the sea and its many forms of life originated through the spilling of a calabash which had been filled with water and bones. Man and woman first entered the world from two sealed caves, which were normally secured by a Guardian Spirit who one day failed in his duties. The inefficient Guardian was severely punished for his lack of attention by being converted into stone.

With the human couple there also escaped the sun, the medium and symbol of fertility. The Arawak account of man's first disobedience seems to be linked up with the ideas of sex and fertility, at least in a symbolic way. Man was forbidden to 'look at' the sun; that is, he must not involve himself in its reproductive and energizing power. Those who disobeyed this injunction and 'looked at' the sun were immediately transformed into some lower form of life, such as an animal, a bird, a tree or a rock. The folk-lore of the Arawaks was full of metamorphic myths wherein an aetiological story would be invented to explain the sound or the appearance of some form of life.

For the Arawaks everything was living, and the only real duty in this life-chain was that of survival. Humans, animals and things were measured only by survival value, and one was not 'better' than another in terms of spirituality or intellectual achievement. Such 'panontism' can lead to respect for all life; equally it can result in the cruel struggle for the survival of the fittest.

The indwelling spirits, or *zemes* (also *zemis*), which pervaded everything, could converse with the people, pass on messages to them from the gods, and also guide their public and private lives. According to the Arawaks all the evils of man's experience, including bereavement and sickness, were caused by the anger of the *zemes*, who had been aroused by man's stupidities and follies. It was, in consequence, important to placate the *zemes* at all times, but in particular on certain ritualistic and public occasions. Festivals, organized by a priestly hierarchy who were held to be responsible for the health, happiness and fertility of the whole society, were held in their honour. During festivals the Arawaks dressed up in all their colourful finery, including shells, feathers and beads, and painted themselves in symbolic and ritualistic ways.

Throughout their festivals the Arawaks used to sing and dance as they offered gifts of meat and bread to the *zemes*. After the gifts of food had been made, offerings of natural objects were made and these were ceremonially blessed by the priests. It was assumed that the *zemes* were pleased with the presents offered to them, and that their acceptance implied health and prosperity for the future. Once all the ceremonies and festivals were over the priests would distribute the gifts to the people. All such objects now possessed a special power, the equivalent of the Polynesian *mana,* which made them fetish objects; and they would be used by the people and by the priests until the next annual festival as 'guardians', or charismatic objects, against the assaults of nature, such as hurricanes, fires and accidents. Throughout all the ceremonies the priest, shaman, or witch-doctor, acted as an intermediary between the people, whom he represented, and the *zemes*; and, indeed, the weight of responsibility for healing the diseases of crops, animals and people lay upon him.

In their healing processes the priests used herbs and herbal decoctions which undoubtedly had medicinal qualities and curative powers. But the medicine-men also employed trickery in their healings – if trickery is the right word in this context. These healers, the only doctors the Arawaks had, were among the pioneers of the psychotherapists who not only have to diagnose a considerable amount of psychosomatic sickness but also have to use a psychological approach in the cure. According to the priest the illness of an individual was initially caused by a *zeme* who had probably introduced an alien substance into the body of the man; and at least part of the cure was to blow tobacco over the patient, and the whole ritual was concluded by kneading the affected area and removing, by a clever piece of sleight of hand, some small object from the patient's body. Sometimes it was assumed that a *zeme* had in fact possessed the patient and that it was necessary to persuade the *zeme* to leave. This view of demon-possession as the cause of sickness was not novel, for 'unclean spirits' were the accepted cause of illness in Palestine at the time of Jesus.

The Arawaks believed that the souls of those who had led a worthy life went to Coyaba, the equivalent of heaven or paradise. This was a land of peace and comfort from which all the dread accidents of earthly life were permanently absent. There was no pain, sickness or death; no drought, hurricane or warfare; everything in Coyaba reflected the joy, laughter and happiness of a carefree existence punctuated by feasting and dancing. We know very little of the actual burial rites of the Arawaks, except that cave-burial was favoured and that the dead were often carefully preserved in pottery bowls.

It is very likely that the Arawaks took a view similar to that of the Caribs, namely that not all souls went to heaven, but only those that were truly worthy. The Arawaks were fundamentally an honest people who despised the thief as much as the Caribs deprecated the coward. In this connexion the *zemes* bore a strong resemblance to the ghosts or spirits of the dead of the North American Indians, referred to by Longfellow as *jeebis*:

> But the ghost, the Jeebi in him,
> Thought and felt as Pau-Puk-Keewis,
> Still lived on as Pau-Puk-Keewis.

Thus, sometimes at least, the ghost of the Indian lived on in the world, and behaved just as the individual did during his life in the flesh. And, just like Pau-Puk-Keewis, he could be a merry mischief-maker, making life very uncomfortable for others. It is probable that the Arawaks felt they were involved with their ancestors through these residual *zemes*, or ghosts, which had not earned a resting-place in Coyaba. The *zemes* were responsible for much of the evil that men suffered, and they were amenable only to the magic of the medicine-man, who at times acted as an exorcist.

It is clear from the researches of the anthropologist Maya Deren that the aboriginal cult of the *zemes* links very strongly with the cult of the Ghede in Haiti. Ghede is the god of the dead and is the dark figure which is present at the meeting of the dead and the living. The cult of the *zemes* has also contributed to the cult of the complex deity Baron Samedi, who is the Lord of the Cemetery and of the magic related to the dead and the cross-roads, the major expression of which is the *zombie*. Probably both the words Samedi and zombie are derived from *zemi*. Many of the Arawak beliefs about *zemes* are identifiable with Haitian beliefs about *zombies* – soulless bodies used as slaves. In passing it is interesting to note that the Kongo word for a fetish was *zumbi*, whilst in the Cumina cult the ancestral spirits are sometimes referred to as *zombies*.

The cult of Cumina, or Kumona, will be discussed in a later chapter when some of the religious cult remnants still to be traced in Jamaican culture are considered. It is worth noting here, however, that Ivy Baxter sees in the Cumina a trace of connection with the Arawak Indians, and she refers in her book to the *cumana* in the Arawak Venezuelan region of South America.

Chapter 3
The Peoples of Jamaica

The motto of Jamaica is: 'Out of Many – One People', and Jamaica is indeed an amalgam of different groups and races.

On 12 October, 1492, Christopher Columbus landed on one of the islands of the Bahamas called by the Indians Guanahani, and he renamed it San Salvador, or Holy Saviour. On his second voyage to the Caribbean he learned about the island of Jamaica from Indians in Cuba; and on 3 May, 1494, he arrived at St Ann's Bay on the north coast. On 4 May he annexed the island for King Ferdinand and Queen Isabella of Spain and then sailed to Cuba. Jamaica was not fully taken over by the Spaniards until 1509, and in 1540 the island was presented by the King of Spain to the family of Columbus as a personal estate which it could develop as it saw fit.

At no time did the Spaniards really make a success of colonizing Jamaica, which was used mainly as a base for further exploits in the Caribbean area. They did very little to develop the country's resources. The Spaniards treated the Arawak Indians brutally, and those who did not die from smallpox and other diseases were maltreated, tortured, starved and sometimes callously killed for sport. The condition of these humiliated Amerindians was such that thousands committed suicide and murdered their children rather than suffer mutilation by the Spaniards.

During the late sixteenth century disturbances in the Iberian peninsula resulted in a flow of European immigrants into Jamaica. In 1580 King Philip II of Spain annexed Portugal, and persecuted Jews in particular fled to the island, where they referred to themselves as 'Portugals'. In this way they were able for some time to conceal the fact that they were Jews who had escaped the net of the Inquisition, and they practised their faith in secret.

The Spaniards' position in Jamaica was always insecure and it is estimated that at the beginning of the seventeenth century there were probably no more than 1,500 Spaniards on the island. They had, however, brought with them some of their own negro slaves, most of whom they had obtained from Africa and had used in Spain before transplanting them to the West Indies.

On 10 May, 1655, Admiral William Penn and General Robert Venables landed at Passage Fort and marched to Spanish Town. The

Spaniards soon realized their inability to withstand the English and surrendered; they were then ordered to leave the island. The Spaniards freed their slaves, and then escaped to the north coast of the island and sailed for Cuba. Such was the identity between the negro slaves and their Spanish owners that the former considered themselves the natural enemies of the English. These freed slaves, and other slaves who ran away from their owners and joined them from time to time, were referred to as Maroons, probably from the Spanish *cimarron*, meaning 'wild, untamed'. The Maroons spent their time hunting wild pig and plundering estates, as well as engaging in guerrilla warfare against the English.

Despite all the efforts of the English to suppress the Maroons they presented a formidable obstacle to peaceful settlement in the new English colony. The colonists were dogged by fevers and famine, epidemics and ambushes; and eventually they were driven to eating almost anything they could find, including dog, rat and horse meat, as well as lizards. Cromwell tried to alleviate the situation of an ever-decreasing white population by sending out a thousand Irish girls and some Scotsmen. Planters were also being attracted to Jamaica from Barbados, Bermuda and New England. It was clear, however, that the actual working of the land was too arduous and enervating a task for most white people. In 1664, therefore, a large number of slaves was transported to the West Indies to work the land; these were euphemistically referred to as 'predials', or farm-workers. This marked the real beginning of an ever-expanding slave trade, in which captured Africans were bought and sold like cattle and herded into ships and living accommodation in such a way that they died like flies from epidemics, hunger and despair.

In 1670, by the Treaty of Madrid, Jamaica was officially ceded by the Spanish to England, and in 1674 some 1,200 settlers came from Surinam, or Dutch Guiana, on the north coast of South America. They began sugar planting. By the turn of the century there must have been over 50,000 people in Jamaica, of very mixed race and nationality; so that during the first forty-five years of occupation by the English there had been a considerable expansion of both population settlement and land cultivation.

There were three broad divisions in the population: whites who were property and plantation owners; whites who were virtually slaves – deported criminals, fugitives from justice and indentured servants; and negro slaves from Africa who could never hope for freedom, but who could simply look forward to a life of debilitating work, poor and inadequate food, and torture. In addition, there were the Maroons living an isolated existence in the interior; and there were those with Spanish or Arawak blood in their veins, though by now there could have been no pure Arawak Indians left. In order to deal with the guerrilla menace of the Maroons some Mosquito Indians were imported from Nicaragua in 1738 because of their prowess in tracking. Finally, the conflict with the French, which was brought to a conclusion in 1782, probably resulted in French prisoners being brought to Port Royal to swell the Jamaican population. There were also some French-speaking refugees from Haiti.

In 1807 the slave trade between Africa and Jamaica was officially abolished by the English Parliament, which meant that after 1 March, 1808, it became illegal to transport any more slaves to Jamaica. This brought an end to a very substantial trade; it has been conservatively estimated that, from the time when Jamaica came into the hands of the English until the abolition of the trade, over one million human beings were imported from Africa as slaves. In 1807 there were some 319,350 slaves in the colony.

On 28 August, 1833, the Abolition of Slavery Act was passed, which enacted that all slave children under six years of age should be set free immediately, that any children born after that date would be born free, and that there should be a six-years' period of apprenticeship for freed slaves from 1834 to 1840. When the apprenticeship system was inaugurated by the Governor, all religious buildings of every denomination were open for divine service and they were packed. But the apprenticeship system was not a success, and it was ended on 1 August, 1838.

By 1841, because a very large number of the freed slaves had contracted out of working for their former masters, labour had to be sought elsewhere. Between 1834 and 1865, over 11,000 free African immigrants settled in Jamaica, which far exceeded the number of the indentured labourers who were imported from India over this period. Other immigrants arrived from Germany, Scotland and Ireland, but many of them soon fell victims to the rigours of the tropical climate. Those who survived very quickly found work other than the hard labouring on the estates, for which they had originally come, so that the really pressing problem of 'predials' was not completely solved. As the number of immigrants from Africa fell away, the most important labour immigrations to Jamaica became those from India and China; those from India began in 1845 and continued until 1917, during which time about 33,000 Indians settled on the island. Between 1860 and 1893 some 5,000 Chinese also arrived. So that today, whilst the largest percentage of Jamaicans are of African descent, there is a multiplicity of nationalities represented on the island.

Chapter 4
The African Origins of Jamaican Slaves

There are several popular myths about the continent of Africa; for example, there still persists the myth that 'darkest Africa', or the 'dark Continent', was rescued from abysmal savagery and cannibalism by an enlightened and philanthropic civilization. In fact, much of the inter-tribal warfare in Africa was no more savage than the perpetual international struggles and intrigue in Europe; whilst the social and political systems of Europe's past could hardly be regarded as much of an advance on some of the involved hierarchical systems in evidence in some parts of Africa.

There is a fundamental similarity of African and European cultures. They share an ancient, common pool of culture, and the manifest differences are more superficial than real, particularly when one considers the great gulfs that separate African culture from (say) that of the Australian aborigines, the Malays, or even the Japanese. This is not to suggest that every African negro who was taken to Jamaica had been Europeanized, or that he accepted European culture. It means that such terms as 'savage', 'ignorant', 'warlike', 'primitive' and so forth, may be as inappropriate when applied to African slaves as when applied to European slaves – or perhaps one should say no more appropriate. All such terms are, of course, relative, and it is very much a matter of debate whether it is more 'civilized' to fight with gunpowder and shot or with spears and arrows. In any consideration of the origins of the slave population of Jamaica it is important to note that it is inaccurate to label them all in a blanket way as poor and ignorant, if not subhuman, savages.

The ancestors of the negroes in the West Indies, and in Jamaica in particular, came from a very wide area of Africa. It is true that the largest numbers were recruited from West Africa; but West Africa was, as it still is, a very mixed as well as large society. In addition, many of the slaves actually bought and sold in West Africa may have come from as far north as the country of the Berbers and Tuaregs; from as far east as Nubia, Sudan and the island of Madagascar; and from as far south as the Congo. F.G. Cassidy and R.B. Le Page demonstrate, in their *Dictionary of Jamaican English,* that there are words in current Jamaican English whose origins are to be found in over forty languages or dialects of Africa; and many of these linguistic vestiges are connected with religious beliefs and ceremonies.

Another myth or misconception to be disposed of is concerned with slavery itself. Slavery was not an evil introduced into Africa by the European white man, however much he may have aggravated and exploited it. Slavery was a long established, and in some ways sophisticated and ritualized, African institution. There were many categories of slaves; some were tribesmen who had been captured in inter-tribal warfare, and who had to serve their new chiefs and masters in domestic or menial tasks, or become a part of the retinue of porters of a powerful king. For example, when the Emperor of Mali, Mansa Musa, left his capital on the banks of the Upper Niger to go on a pilgrimage to Mecca in 1324, he took with him five hundred slaves.

Slaves certainly had domestic value in helping with household work or as labourers in the field. They had an additional economic value in a double sense: they represented a part of the wealth of their owner who would count his slaves in much the same way as he might count his cattle, or perhaps his wives. But, like money, slaves also had some exchange value. One might buy goods with gold, cowrie shells, or slaves, and in the African mart the value of a slave would appreciate or depreciate like gold itself, according to the state of the market, and supply and demand. There were monopolies which rigorously controlled the trade in slaves, as, for example, in Nigeria where a priestly society, or 'oracle', controlled and organized the trade up and down the region of the River Niger. A tribesman who suddenly disappeared was said to have been 'eaten by the oracle', that is, he had been captured and sold into slavery.

Slaves were not all of equal standing, nor were they all captives of inter-tribal warfare. Some were criminals who were kept in domestic slavery as a form of punishment; some slaves were regarded almost as kinsmen, as members of the household or family group. There was also the possibility of advancement within a large household, where a slave might be put in charge of some part or area of the household. Slaves would, like their masters, tend to become specialized, usually at the lowest levels of domestic activity, although noblemen and their sons who had been captured in war by another tribe might sometimes find themselves in a favoured position in the realm of their captors. The situation, however, was different if they were sold to white men.

Not all Africans are, or have been, negroes; some are Hamites or Caucasians, and others are Bushmen. For several centuries before the Arabs became involved in African slavery, however, there was a tendency for the slave population to become increasingly negroid. The Tuaregs developed a hierarchical or caste system in which there were noblemen at the top, vassals as a middle class, and slaves at the lowest level. These latter were negroes, and as time passed the vassal class became increasingly negro also.

Among the Ashanti, slaves had precisely stated obligations, duties and rights; they could marry, were permitted to own property or even a lower grade slave, and they were acceptable as witnesses in lawsuits. According to their position in a particular household they might even become heirs to their masters. Many Ashanti slaves who eventually arrived in Jamaica must have been bewildered not simply by their new environment and work, but also by their complete lack of personal rights or established legal relationships.

The first Muslim Arabs entered Egypt in A.D. 639 and by the end of the century they had overrun the African continent north of the Sahara. They established trading relations with Nubia and made an agreement that, if the Nubians would send 360 slaves to Egypt each year and would guarantee freedom of access and worship to Arab traders, the latter would respect their independence and trade with them. The Arabs extended their influence as far west as the empires of Kenem-Bornu, Hausa and Ghana; and as Islam spread so there developed – probably about the twelfth century – a full-scale slave *trade,* as distinct from a domestic institution of slavery.

By about 1445 there was in Portugal a steady market in slaves from Africa, and before the end of the fifteenth century there were several provinces in Portugal which had a population composed of more negro slaves than native Portuguese. The Portuguese established some coastal forts at Elmina on the Gold Coast in order to ward off any other European opportunists who might seek to share their trade in gold. In the early sixteenth century they made what was for them a break-through in the trade with human ivory. They began to supply the ever-pressing need for labour in the New World. But as more and more nations became interested in America and the Caribbean in the seventeenth century so the demand for slaves became greater. West Africa gradually became the centre of a world slave trade, and the French, English and Dutch were all involved in it.

Dispersal and transit camps, known as slave 'factories', were set up on the coast, where slaves were bought and sold for gold or firearms, and eventually put on board ship for transport to Jamaica. The largest proportion of Jamaican negroes are probably of Ashanti and Fanti origin. They were usually referred to as Koromantyns (Coromantees, Coromantins etc.) from the name of the town and settlement area of the Gold Coast where many of the slaves transported in the seventeenth and early eighteenth centuries came from. The Koromantyns were noted for their bravery, their stubbornness and their leadership, and many of them were later to be found among the Maroons, leading them into further revolt. Another tribal group strongly represented among the slaves was the Ibos or Eboes, who came from the Bight of Benin; their skins were lighter than the Ashantis' and they were sometimes referred to as 'Red Eboes', although they were more yellow than red. The Ibos were looked down upon by the Koromantyns who regarded them as lazy and cowardly, although it was held that Ibo women worked both willingly and well.

Other tribes represented among the Jamaican negro slaves were the Tiv (southeast Nigeria), the Hausa and Yoruba (Nigeria), the Fula and Wolof (Gambia), the mainly Muslim Mandingo (Sierra Leone) and the Twi (Ghana). Large numbers also came from Dahomey, whose coastal factory was at Whydah, and whose chief tribes were the Ewe and the Fon. By the time that the slave trade came to an end in 1807-1808 an increasing number was being imported from the Congo and Angola. The wide spread of dialects which were brought from Africa to Jamaica was mentioned earlier, and it was from this collection of languages, as well as from English, that Jamaican Creole was gradually developed.

Despite the great variety of tribal origins of these negro slave immigrants, they all shared certain general African cultural characteristics, as well as the unhappy lot which helped to bind them together as a people in captivity. A study of the Ashanti, for example, gives the lie to the concept of the primitive African savage being moved from one form of animal existence to another. The Ashanti were a proud group who had, by the eighteenth century, developed into a single feudal state ruled over by the King of all the Ashantis. Their military system was founded upon the qualities of heroism and courage, and these were virtues which they sought to incorporate into their daily activity. Only the recollection of their heritage could have kept many of these courageous Ashanti slaves alive in the conditions of labour and torture meted out to them by their plantation overseers.

Chapter 5
Some Aspects of African Religion

Much of current Jamaican culture and religion is African in origin, and sometimes represents a deliberate attempt at some sort of recreation of an African life-style. It is important, therefore, to examine certain aspects of African culture, not in any highly systematic way, but to bring out those elements which are most relevant to Jamaican development.

Animism

Animism is the belief that the phenomena of nature are somehow endowed with personal life, and it is a concept which is shared by primitive societies throughout the world. But this concept of endowment with life varies from one group to another. The writer recalls watching with some fascination members of the Motuan tribe in Papua walking about in the evening, and suddenly putting their arms around the slender trees in order to 'breathe' with them. The Motuans believed that, in this way, they were sharing the life of the trees and that they were thereby regenerating themselves after the labours of the day. Amongst the Bantu there is the idea of *ntu*, or cosmic force, which pervades and permeates all phenomena. This term *ntu* is the verbal root of a great variety of elements, including *muntu*, or human being, and *bantu* which is the plural of *muntu*. This cosmic force or intelligence is located in every single thing *(kintu)*; it is the essential dimension of time and place *(hantu)*, and it informs the very modality of life *(kuntu)*.

This permeation of life in all its variety and dimensions in Africa finds a parallel in the Melanesian concept of *mana*, the North American Indian *orenda* and *manitu*, as well as the Australian aboriginal *arungquiltha*. Through this strange, mysterious, sacred force all things become one; through the *ntu*, *mana* and *orenda* which interpenetrate all things there exists a numinous level of life to which everything ministers and of which they are all a part.

But if all life is fundamentally one it is also represented in a discrete fashion – there are people, animals, trees, rivers and stones, and they behave in a great variety of ways. This differentiation of phenomena is accounted for by the existence within each separate thing of an anima, a soul, phantom, ghost or double. Hence, in addition to the pervasive *ntu*, there are also multitudes of these spiritual beings or elements both in objects and also floating free. The Ashanti, for example, believe in the existence of *mmoatia*, or troublesome spirits, which may annoy people, throw stones at them or even inhabit them. They are in the nature of poltergeists which may be 'caught' or, if necessary, exorcised. As we shall see later, the belief in *duppies,* or harmful spirits, is virtually universal in Jamaica and is the equivalent of this concept of *mmoatia.*

Among the Ashanti there is the belief that everything possesses a *sunsum,* or soul. Thus, even a stool may possess the *sunsum* of the nation, and the nation's very power, health, bravery and welfare may be enshrined and embodied in this stool. If it were to be stolen or destroyed then the Ashanti would sicken and lose their power and vitality. Similarly, a man's sunsum, which has been injured by some other *sunsum,* will sicken and die. Oddly enough this word has survived in Jamaican Creole, although its use is somewhat rare. It refers particularly to the force of the emotions within the individual, and it is still customary in Jamaica to 'throw words at the moon'. It is accepted that one may tell the moon the most slanderous things about another person within his hearing, and yet be in no danger of any court action. It is not the speaker who really slanders, but 'Him moon talk'. This is a way of cooling one's *sunsum* and of providing it with an element of contentment and satisfaction.

Thus, in the animism of the African, the entire realm of nature has been endowed with personal life; and every tree or plant, every river or stone, becomes a source of energy or power which may be used, abused, offended or destroyed. For example, a ritual has to be employed to propitiate even the *sunsum* of the tree before it is cut down to make a ritual stool.

Hierarchy of Gods

Among the Yoruba there has been a fairly clear conception of the order and function of the deities. Perhaps not surprisingly the gods considered to be of greatest importance have been those of fertility and vegetation, for they antedated the establishment of the solar gods. It is not easy, however, to disentangle the real evolutionary development of native ideas from the later patterning of Western rationalization. The Western mind always seeks to impose some organization or order upon what is very often virtually chaotic or without any logical structure. In the primitive natural world all things grow and develop as there is a felt need, however apparently irrational or non-rational; and the result is not always amenable to orderly arrangement.

At some point the Yoruba certainly began to think in terms of a being who 'owned' the sky, and who, as lord of the sky, attained to supreme importance. This being, Awlawrun or Olorun, although certainly personalized, never appeared in sculptured form. He is not a god who can be contained in the way that many other gods are – the sky is boundless.

The *orisha*, or hierarchy of gods below Awlawrun, act as function gods who mediate between the lord of the sky and mankind. In this sense they are similar to any other pantheon in which the lesser gods represent the myriad eyes of the supreme god watching over all and meeting men's needs. Shango, for example, is the lightning god and special symbolic and sacred dances are performed in his honour. Ogun is a god with a great variety of occupation – he is the patron god of hunters, warriors, blacksmiths and even snakecharmers; he is also god of war and of craftsmen. Okum is one of the agricultural deities, representing Awlawrun in a fertility function.

In parts of Central and West Africa, Awlawrun is also called Nyame, which signifies a fundamental force or power; whilst amongst the Ashanti the name Nyankonpon is also used. In Jamaica this latter name survives in the Maroon form of Accompong, the name of their headquarters in the Cockpit country. It was also probably used as a personal name by Koromantyn negroes. In East Africa this supreme being was also known as Mulungu, or 'the one who makes order', and he was regarded as the creator of all things who brought order out of chaos.

Among the Akan-Ashanti there are lesser gods called *abosom*. An *obosom* is neither a thing nor a mere wandering ghost, but a personalized being with a clear function. The Ashanti chief and his elders had to go through a ceremony of 'drinking the gods'. The potion actually drunk was contained in a phial, and was 'holy water' which had been rendered potent by being poured over a god, or a sacred stool, and then mixed with rum. If the drinker was deceitful the potion had power to destroy him.

Amongst some Africans there is a belief in reincarnation and ancestor worship. The main concept behind this seems to be a logical one of continuity, and many Africans have for a long time appealed to the spiritual power of their ancestors as a part of this pattern of continuance. Some of these ancestral spirits *(samanfo)* are accepted as gods for whom regular ceremonies are performed, to whom prayers are said and offerings of meat, vegetables and blood are made. The ancestors are viewed as beings who, having originally emanated from the great sky-god, have at length returned to their creator, but who also act as intermediaries who are more accessible to the worshipper because related to him during their earthly existence. Thus the ideas of god's transcendence and immanence find a meeting-place in the persons of the ancestors.

Thus there is a sequence in the hierarchy of the gods and spirits from Awlawrun, Nyankonpon, or Nyame, through Ala the Earth Mother, and through the *orisha* or function gods and the *abosom* or lesser gods, down to the *samanfo* or ancestral spirits. All have their special role to play in the social solidarity of the tribal group and in the efficient working of the nation.

Folklore and Myth

The folklore and mythology of the Africans are amongst the richest in the world and they provide many parallels with those of other continents. In the Jamaican context, much of the folklore of the Ashanti, in particular, has survived, or been recreated in one form or another.

The similarity of many of the folk stories, legends and myths in different parts of Africa may, it is true, be due to similar responses of different groups to common questions and problems – how the world began, how evil came into the world, and how man was created. It seems likely, however, that such folk cycles were disseminated throughout the continent by means of the institution of slavery and the slave trade. The folk-tales of the Ashanti and the Hausa, for example, would seem to have a common source.

Many of the Ashanti folk-tales represent a form of catharsis and psychological release from the unknown and inexplicable terrors of nature that surround them. In the telling of the traditional stories of their tribe almost anything can become a matter of ridicule, jest and laughter – from the great sky-god Nyame or Nyankonpon, to the tribal king or chief and anyone or anything within the tribe, including such dread and painful diseases as syphilis, yaws and leprosy. Within the framework of the folk-tale the most sacred things lose their sanctity and tabu quality, if only during the recital of the story.

The teller of the story is fully safeguarded from the wrath of the gods, spirits or chiefs by the somewhat naive introduction to his tale: 'We do not really mean, we do not really mean that what we are going to say is true'. And to clinch the matter, so that there is no danger whatsoever of the lampooning episode being taken seriously, the story is concluded with the statement: 'This is my story which I have told, and if it be sweet, or if it be not sweet, some you may accept as true and the rest you may praise me for telling it'. In this way the raconteur, like the jester-figure, could get away with a great deal of ridicule of his master's weaknesses, such as jealousy, greed or bombast. By such means all men are brought together through their peccadilloes, and identity is found with the lesser gods.

Many of the Ashanti tales are an attempt to draw a moral from certain forms of behaviour. Often animals take the place of humans – perhaps to take some of the sting out of the attack on human frailty. The choice of animals may also be the result of vestiges of clan totemism, and many of the tales reveal a sense of identity with certain animals and insects and their characteristics. Human qualities are personified not only in animals but also in plants and fruits. A large proportion of the tales, however, attempt to explain the origin of certain facts and forms of behaviour. Some are, additionally, etymological tales, for example, 'How it came about that when Nwansana the fly settles on Kraman the dog, he snaps at it, Kam! Kam!'

More generally the collection of folk-tales of the Akan-Ashanti is known as *Anansesem* or spider-stories. Ananse is, in the Ashanti myth cycle, a sobriquet of Nyankonpon, the supreme creator sky-god, and he is the central figure of a large proportion of these tales. He appears to have a multiplicity of functions, many of which seem to be contradictory. He is the originator and dispenser of all wisdom; he is the inventor of the sky-god's stories (Nyankonsem), which henceforth become spider-stories; he is the servant of the sky-god to bring diseases among the tribe. He is also the agent for the scattering of personality traits among the tribesmen, such as the characteristics of *aferehyia'-boa* ('the-take-a-year-to-do-anything creature'), and *onam-bere-bere-be-ko-Aburokyire* ('he-walks-very-slowly-but he-will-reach-the-land-of-the-white-men-far-away'). Sometimes Ananse is the soul-washer to the sky-god, whilst at other times he is a thief, a liar, and an unconscionable trickster.

The trickster frequently figures in African folklore and mythology, sometimes in the form of a spider and sometimes as a chameleon. The Twi word for the chameleon, *abosom-akotere,* epitomizes the changing, tricking, deceiving roles of the lesser gods. Ananse spins a web between heaven and earth, and by means of this network god can come down to man and man can reach up to god. But man's separation from god is not completely bridged by this web, for everything depends upon the nature and character of Ananse who can trick both god and man. This is, like so many of the trickster figures throughout the races of the world, an attempt by man to come to terms with the problems of sin, evil, disease, disaster and determinism. The messenger of the gods becomes a bringer of both good and evil; he is both a satan and a saviour, a deceiver and a helper; he is a devouring monster catching unsuspecting man within his web as well as a mediator assisting man in his perilous ascent to god. This concept of god as the devourer, eating his own creation, is found in religions throughout the world; and it expresses very forcefully the ambivalence which man feels about the nature of god, his own fear of god or the gods, and his desire for some form of identity or union with the cosmic forces.

Among the Ashanti, Ananse is represented not merely as a trickster figure but also as a ghost-hunter and a washer of souls for Nyankonpon. He acts, therefore, as a guardian for man, hunting and warding off the ghosts which oppress him; and he also stands between man and god, washing souls so that they might be worthy to appear before him. Thus, the labyrinthine web of the spider is, in a very real sense, a symbol of the sky-god's inextricable weaving of man's pattern of life, and of man's total inability to avoid the voracity of Nyankonpon. Ananse, supported by his children, Ntikuma, Tikononkono (Big-big-head), Afudotwe-dotwe (Belly-like-to-burst) and Nyiwankonfea (Thin-shanks), and his wife Aso or Konnore, is both god and man and expresses fully man's weaknesses as well as his strength and guile. Nor is there anything ideal about his family relationships, which are very much a reflection of tribal family behaviour. Ntikuma sometimes supports his father in his activities, but at other times he delights in opposing him and tricking him, even in the presence of the sky-god.

We shall see later on, when we come to discuss some of the folk-tales of modern Jamaica, that many of their ideas about the function of Ananse (or Anancy), the Spider, reflect Ashanti folklore.

Magic, Sorcery and Witchcraft

There is an Ashanti proverb which says, 'A witch is passing by! A witch is passing by! But if you are not a witch you do not turn to look!' The term *obayifo* is used of a witch or a vampire who delights in sucking the blood of children, and who can enter animals and cause them to destroy people. Witches are held responsible for a variety of activities, from causing death and disease to bringing bad luck and misfortune to people and performing acts of sheer magic. The term *obi okomfo* is used as a name for a fetish priest who produces a variety of magic by means of a fetish.

The Ashanti and kindred tribes, that is, the Twi-speaking groups called Koromantyns by the slave-dealers, were exported from the Gold Coast to British rather than Spanish or French colonies. The reason suggested for this is that, on account of the Koromantyn disposition to rebel, the British markets were the only ones open to them. Thus *obayi,* or the practice of witchcraft among these tribes, was taken to Jamaica and became the esoteric possession of the slaves which they did not share with the whites, but which nevertheless they could use for their personal advantage against their owners. The word *obayi* became corrupted into *obeah, obiah* or *obia,* and the form *obi* was also used.

It is interesting to note, however, that other forms of witchcraft exist in Africa and that some of these have been transmitted to the Caribbean area – particularly to Haiti – and have been developed into a very different sort of cult. Ophiolatry, or snake-worship, existed in West Africa, particularly in Dahomey and Southern Nigeria, for a very long time. From about 1725 onwards slaves who were shipped to the West Indies from Whydah took python worship, or the *voodoo* cult, with them; and this was reinforced by the serpents which they found in Haiti. But whilst the cult and the term *voodoo* and its variants *(vodu, voudoun)* exist in Haiti, and in some of the surrounding islands, such as La Gonave, they have not survived in Jamaica, and it seems improbable that this particular form of witchcraft or religion ever took root there. Such intermediate forms as *myalism* are best considered in the context of Jamaica itself, and we shall look at such elements in some detail later.

In Africa the practice of sorcery and witchcraft has always been accompanied by a collection of dirt, animal entrails, blood, teeth, fowl's feet, feathers and often human or animal excrement. By means of these ingredients there is an attempt to attract the spiritual forces of nature in order to control events, human behaviour, and such things as health and fertility. The various 'operators' of magic, sorcery and witchcraft are clearly distinguished among the Ashanti – there is the priest who is concerned with normal religious ritual which takes place at specific periods during the year; there is the medicine-man who works with the use of the fetish in order to perform his sympathetic magic to cure the sick in body and mind; there is the witch-doctor whose main function is concerned with the control and exorcism of evil monsters; and there is the priest of witchcraft who is largely concerned with the offering of gifts, such as rice and groundnut soup, to the spirits of dead ancestors.

In general, *obayi* or witchcraft has been regarded as antisocial magic and its practitioners as devotees of evil and black arts, but all the other classes of priests and medicine-men were performing a positive function in society, assisting in its health and general well-being. Drought and infertility were problems for primitive society without technical and artificial means to combat them; hence much of the African ritual has been associated with overcoming the anger of the gods, or the hero-gods, associated with the production of rain and the prolongation of fertility. The African has always felt that the spirits, gods, fairies and imps could be influenced, placated and cajoled by rituals, sacrifices and the activities of particular types of intermediary such as the rain-maker or rain-stopper, the medicine-man or the witch-doctor.

It is important, when considering the spiritualistic developments in Jamaican religion, to note that the African has always appeared to believe in some sort of spirit-possession. This is not something that all are subject to; some individuals seem to have psychic faculties more highly developed than others. Such powers are believed to come from some familiar spirit which has attached itself to the individual, and which may prophesy through him, or heal, or produce some other form of psi-phenomena or paranormal activity. Some of these 'possessed' individuals go into trance states and appear to be different personalities altogether.

Chapter 6
Treatment of Slaves in the Caribbean

In any consideration of the treatment of slaves in Jamaica we are inevitably concerned with the way in which slaves were dealt with generally in the New World and, of course, more particularly in the area of the Caribbean. It is sometimes argued that the brutality towards slaves during the eighteenth century, when discipline in both the British Navy and Army was very harsh, has been exaggerated. As late as 1823, for example, a British soldier in Jamaica was given 900 lashes of the cat-o'-nine-tails for using language of a rebellious nature. In many European countries theft was still, in certain circumstances, a capital offence. We are here, however, much more concerned with the social effects of brutality in general upon slaves, with the position of slaves in society itself, and with their rights compared with other human beings, than with specific punishments for particular crimes – although even here it is clear that they did not always receive the same consideration as their white masters or overseers.

It is generally agreed that the Iberians and the North-West Europeans treated their slaves differently. Writing in 1910, Sir Henry Johnston claimed that 'slavery under the flag of Portugal or of Spain was not a condition without hope, a life in hell, as it was for the most part in the British West Indies and above all Dutch Guiana and the Southern United States'. Slaves in the British West Indies were virtually denied the privileges of Christianity. In 1834, Mrs Carmichael (the wife of a planter) complained of the lack of Christian instruction of the negro population. But she did not appear to be any great supporter of the 'privileges of Christianity' in any wider sense, for she regarded the 'injudicious harangues made in parliament' and the theories of the Society for the Suppression of Slavery as impracticable.

The codification of Spanish Common Law began in about 1250, and in *Las Siete Partidas* not only the duties of the slave but also his rights and the obligations of his master towards him were legally defined. There was, in addition, a recognition from early times that the slave was another human being with a full human nature. In 1622 a Caribbean Catholic Synod produced sanctions which were regarded as law, and which provided in some detail the sort of chastisement which should be dealt out to masters who impeded their slaves from participating in Mass or from receiving religious instruction on Feast days.

In 1789 the Spaniards fully coded and regulated the legal position of their negro slaves in the New World generally. By this code masters had to encourage Christian marriage between slaves and were not permitted to countenance 'unlawful intercourse' between the two sexes. The code clearly envisaged the possibility of a slave's purchase of his freedom by instalments; when the last payment had been made the slave became his own master. This manumission, known by the Spaniards as *coartacion,* somehow never seemed to give complete equality, for although manumitted slaves became free under the law they were rarely regarded as better than second-rate citizens. No negro was allowed to carry firearms of any description, and there existed a variety of restrictions regarding dress and behaviour in public and towards their former white masters. In fact, the very word *coartacion* meant a 'limitation' or 'restraint' upon both ownership and freedom.

But the possibility of freedom, however partial and limited, always existed under Spanish and Portuguese rule, whereas the legal position regarding manumission was never quite so clear under British and Dutch rule. Thus, even in the 1820s Mrs Carmichael had apparently never heard of any expressed wish for freedom on the part of slaves in St Vincent. Perhaps the wish had been expressed so often without any positive results that the slaves had given up asking by the time Mrs Carmichael arrived in 1820. She maintained, however, that the old Spanish law had never been changed in Trinidad, and that it was a much milder code than that of any English colony. In Trinidad every slave, 'upon paying his own price at a fair valuation', might, if he so wished, immediately claim his freedom.

Slaves escaping to Cuba to embrace Catholicism were protected by a special royal order of 1733 which was twice reissued. Further, a slave who had been wrongly punished might be freed by a magistrate; in the Portuguese colony of Brazil the fact that a slave was the parent of at least ten children was sufficient for him (or her) to demand freedom. Indeed, the Spanish Code appeared to contain a number of possibilities for manumission quite apart from any payment to masters in order to purchase freedom. For example, cooperation with masters, or with the legal authorities, in certain criminal situations was enough to procure the termination of servitude.

The Spanish Code also had a certain leniency when it came to a question of lawful punishment. It was universally accepted that slaves must be punished adequately for any misdemeanours of which they might be guilty, but at the same time failure to perform their duties must not be penalized by excessive or, by contemporary standards, inhumane punishments. Regard must always be paid to the fact that the slave was not just another chattel, but a person with human rights. Lashes with the cat were limited to twenty-five, and they had to be administered by the master or his steward in such a way as not to cause any contusion or effusion of blood. A slave accused of a crime, even murder, had to be accorded the same rights of prosecution and trial as any free person. A slave might also, in some areas, have the same privileges in relation to holidays and feast days as the rest of society. This applied also in Brazil where slaves were free on all Sundays and public holidays. During those times they might work on their own account to build up capital for their manumission.

One essential feature of the Spanish Code was that every slave had to be fully instructed in the principles of the Roman Catholic faith and its 'necessary truths', in order that he might be baptized within a year of taking up residence in a Spanish colony. Coloured slaves were regarded as people who needed to be brought within the aegis of the Church, and it was considered a duty for all masters of slaves to ensure that the latter became Christians.

Some of the earliest writers on colonization emphasized that both the Spaniards and the Portuguese were the best masters of slaves among the five nations involved in slavery and the slave trade, whilst the British and the Dutch were the worst. Even the French, who are usually regarded as coming somewhere between the two extremes, used to complain that their slaves in Haiti would, if possible, escape to a Spanish dominion where they knew they would receive better treatment. Negroes and mulattos in Spanish colonies were often skilled craftsmen, soldiers, musicians and even priests and judges. All these things were possible to the slave before the abolition of the slave trade and slavery, and it was for this reason (amongst others) that emancipation in Iberian dominions occurred without violence, bloodshed or civil war.

It is, perhaps, easy to see how slavery under a democratic regime could be more inhumane than under a despotic rule. Despotism always sets limits to private property ownership; democracy has tended to grant greater freedom to the individual over his personal property. Thus, under British rule, the slave-master had virtually absolute power of life and death over his slave chattel. Laws that existed which related to slavery were almost entirely to the advantage of the white owners and to the detriment of slaves. Indeed, it took a considerable amount of political, social and religious propaganda to arouse any sort of public conscience in Britain about the plight of slaves. Even the liberality and paternal treatment shown to slaves on the island of Trinidad (which Spain had ceded to Britain in 1802), were almost entirely an inheritance of the Spanish Code rather than any really positive attitude or policy of the British.

One of the interesting features of the development of the population in Jamaica itself is the continued existence of the Maroons, who live mainly in and around the Cockpit country. The Spaniards had taken negro slaves with them to Jamaica prior to 1517, and the original Maroons were negro slaves whom the Spaniards had set free, or who had run away into the interior of the island. They were later joined by groups of Koromantyns who had rebelled against their masters in Clarendon and had escaped into the dense woodland. After considerable warfare, lasting for seventy-six years, and no small expenditure of both life and money, peace was eventually established with Cudjoe, the leader of the Maroons, who were in 1738 guaranteed freedom and were awarded 1,500 acres of land in perpetuity as well as certain wild-pig hunting rights. They were permitted to govern themselves and had their own legal system, except that their chief, or 'Colonel', was not permitted to pass sentence of death on any of them. They were also in future required to assist in the capturing of runaway slaves.

The fact that there were many such runaway slaves is at least an indication that their treatment in Jamaica was hardly on a par with that of their African brethren in Cuba or Brazil. It is, of course, a generalization but it is one which contains a large measure of truth, that whereas the Iberian settlers were concerned mainly to establish homes and cities, the Anglo-Saxon colonists came primarily to develop trade and to get rich as quickly as possible. Certainly English planters were not usually anxious to devote their lives to the development of the British West Indies in any idealistic way; for by and large they were the absentee proprietors of their estates, which were run by harsh overseers seeking to extract the last ounce of gold out of their commission. The planters, living in England and on the Continent, could well afford to be generous and to display their personal liberality to friends and relatives, whilst their wealth was being amassed for them mainly by the slaves – the real plantation workers in Jamaica and elsewhere.

Punishment was an organized and regular part of the life of the plantation and in the early days a planter was able to do very much as he liked with his slaves. Gradually he came under stricter control, as the laws which related to slaves were made less harsh; but the early 'slave code' was very brutal. A slave might have a leg, an ear or an arm cut off for a very minor offence, or he might be severely flogged. In 1781, however, when General Archibald Campbell became Lieutenant-Governor of Jamaica, a law was passed by the House of Assembly making it illegal to punish slaves by any form of mutilation. Planters or overseers found guilty of such conduct were to be severely dealt with. Yet as late as 1830 a female slave was caught, tried and sentenced to life imprisonment with hard labour for absenting herself from her owner's plantation for a period of more than six months.

All forms of assembly were forbidden in Jamaica, largely because of the fear of conspiracy and revolt. Banned gatherings included any attempt at religious meetings. Thus the negro slaves were not in any way encouraged by their masters to involve themselves in religious worship, whether Christian or African. In consequence there was a tendency for only the dark, secret forms of African witchcraft and sorcery to survive, in particular the practice of obeah.

No doubt slave-owners and plantation overseers varied as much as any other class of human being in their regard for others and in their interpersonal relationships. But they were involved in a monetary and trade project which had to succeed, and they themselves were judged by the successful output of the products that they were growing. The system of the absentee proprietor lent itself to the maltreatment of slaves who were often punished for the inefficiency and inadequacy of their overseers. But although some owners were kind and generous, in general slaves in Jamaica were treated harshly; they were made to work extremely hard in very unhealthy conditions, had very little leisure or free time to cultivate their own small plots of land, and were discouraged from any involvement in Christian or any other religious practices.

There was an assumption that a slave was a slave for life, and that his children were slaves 'for all generations'. Anything which might suggest other possibilities, such as eventual freedom and equality with the white races in the sight of God, was quickly suppressed or discouraged. In the main the slaves who rebelled against this sort of treatment were the Koromantyns; whilst those who were largely resigned to their unfavourable lot were the Ibos who were virtually a slave race when they were in Africa. They had become docile, if unwilling, workers, and when they did rebel they organized themselves separately.

In Hausaland, in Northern Nigeria, the Muslim Hausa of Zaria, with their institution of slavery, had developed a society which was relatively homogeneous and highly integrated. In Jamaica, however, a society developed which was both plural and badly integrated. The Hausa had made proper arrangements for the marriages of their slaves, but in the Jamaican slave society no attempt at such provision was made. Indeed, everything possible was done to prevent the mating habits of a 'Christian' society, so that no dignity or sanctity could be afforded the sex relationships of the negro slaves. They were treated as animals, used for occasional mating with their masters or simply for breeding in order to increase the labour stock of their masters. To afford them the dignity of a marriage sanctified in church, or the possibilities of an accepted family situation, would inevitably provide them with a place in society among human beings. They would then certainly get ideas above their station.

There were economic as well as social reasons for this lack of promotion of marriage among slaves. During the long years of slavery the planters or overseers refused to allow their slaves to marry under the aegis of Christian ritual, since this would have encouraged permanent relationships. A master could always get a better price for slaves who were sold separately than for those who were put up for auction as man and wife. Even today, in Jamaica Christian marriage is more of an ideal than an actuality; it represents the consummation not so much of love or desire as of social ambition.

In general, the unity and integration which the Catholic philosophy provided tended to lead to a unified society, and this was reflected in the life of the slave in Spanish colonies. On the other hand, the extreme individualism of Protestant religious views and philosophy unavoidably led to division and lack of social homogeneity. This effect could be seen in British, American and Dutch colonies, and it is reflected in the lack of unity and common purpose in Jamaican life today, and in the burgeoning of highly individual religious sects.

Jamaica has become a happy hunting-ground for every conceivable religious movement, with perhaps the exception of the most sophisticated. The Roman Catholic Church, however temporal its power and secular its interests, has always seen its task as both international and supranational. Where it dominates it tends to bind society together even by its own weakness and internal contradictions. On the other hand, the whole concept and effect of Protestantism is ultimately one of divisiveness and atomization. Protestantism began by doing too little for the slaves: it finished by trying to provide too much – too much, that is, in the way of possible variants of Christian belief. This position is not peculiar to Jamaica or the West Indies; it is, in fact, world-wide, and it found a desperate expression some years ago in the request of certain groups in Papua New Guinea, who pleaded with their government not to allow any more varieties of Christian missionary into their territory, because they no longer knew what Christianity was supposed to be.

Chapter 7
Jamaican Slaves and Christianity

Jamaica was occupied by Juan de Esquivel from Santo Domingo in 1509, and when the first Spanish settlers arrived they began an immediate campaign to convert the native Arawak population to Catholic Christianity. At first they constructed simple churches of wood and straw, which were gradually replaced by much larger and more solid structures of stone. One such church was built at St Ann's Bay, then known as Sevilla Neuva; in addition, religious houses were founded.

The Spanish masters always felt that it was incumbent upon them to instruct their slaves in the Catholic faith; in fact, it was an essential feature of the Spanish Slave Code. But the Amerindian Arawaks were not particularly impressed by the new religion preached to them, since they associated it very closely with the heavy work which they were forced to do for their Spanish conquerors. Moreover, as we have seen, the Arawaks were unable physically to survive the harsh treatment that they received at the hands of the conquistadores, and within a little over a century their population had declined from something in the region of 60,000 to 74.

As the Amerindian population declined so the Spanish settlers became increasingly dependent upon the use of negro slaves who had been steadily imported from Africa since the beginning of the Spanish occupation. But the colony remained poverty-stricken and open to the attacks made repeatedly upon it by privateers and the ever-increasing number of runaway slaves, who frequently ganged up to pillage homes and sack churches. The colonists also suffered considerable damage and loss from hurricanes. In 1655 the islands became a British colony, and in consequence the established Roman Catholic faith and the Spanish way of life were quickly superseded by Protestantism and the current British life-style.

Soon after Charles II (1660-85) came to the British throne he received reports from the Jamaican colony concerning the general lack of religious organization, and the open immorality and uncivilized behaviour of a fair proportion of the British colonists in the island. In consequence he issued instructions that, in addition to rule by martial law, the Church of England was to become established in Jamaica in order, in his own words, 'to discourage vice and debauchery'.

As an increasing number of settlers arrived, and the population of negro slaves increased, the whole question of the morality of the slaves and of slavery itself began to be mooted. For their part, the English planters made it clear that, whatever the Anglican clergy might teach and preach, they did not want the slaves to get any ideas above their station, which was essentially one of total subservience. Nor, moreover, did they want the slave labourers to be worried too much about such sophisticated matters as sexual morality. The planters and their white managers, overseers and attorneys lived lives in which gambling, immorality and heavy drinking seem to have been the main forms of leisure activity. Female slaves were regarded for the most part as chattels to be used by their masters in any way they saw fit, or as the passion took them. In the meantime, the Anglican clergy generally took the path of discretion and exhorted the slaves to please their masters by working hard, and to accept with resignation their earthly lot which, whether predestined by God or not, had somehow devolved upon them.

It has been pointed out that the deliberate exclusion of the Caribbean slaves from the Christian community, to which their masters belonged, created differences of kind between the two groups. This resulted in the exploitation of slaves as real property from which their owners could extract the maximum social economic satisfaction. Unlike the Muslim Hausa, who converted their slaves to Islam, the English colonists in the Caribbean denied their slaves Christianity and treated them as being outside the pale of any Christian or human rights. As a result the response of the slaves themselves was negative, and rebellious crimes became common. In the Jamaican slave-society only the whites were considered to belong to the nation of the mother country, and the social distance between masters and slaves was very carefully maintained. They belonged to two different worlds in which their social institutions (whether of marriage, religion, education, kinship or family) were very differently conceived.

In the eighteenth century the number of Anglican clergy was very small, and there is little doubt that for the most part they accepted that the maintenance of this social distance was a good thing. Some undoubtedly felt that they might be able to do more for their coloured parishioners by not openly opposing and angering the planters and their overseers. Others somewhat naively suggested that if the slaves were converted to Christianity they would become increasingly tractable, so that money spent on the expansion of the Anglican Church would be worthwhile. Edward Long, however, writing in 1774, did not mince his words when he suggested that there were some clerics who were more qualified to retail salt fish, or even to act as boatswains for privateers than to perform the functions of Christian priests.

By about 1820 at least a million slaves had been imported into Jamaica from the West coast of Africa, and out of a population at that date of something like 380,000 it was estimated that at least 310,000, or about 81 per cent, were slaves. And yet, in the *Jamaican Almanac* for 1812, only twenty clergymen of the Church of England were listed; and it became very clear that if the Anglican Church were to become in any sense a force in Jamaican society, or were to give even the most elementary instruction to its flock, whether white or black, the number of resident priests had to be considerably increased. But, in fact, during the next ten years only another dozen clerics were appointed, and it was only in 1825 that a bishop, who was to be responsible for the selection, character and supervision of the clergy, was appointed.

Whilst the Anglican Church did little or nothing to alleviate the plight of the slaves, there were other sects and denominations of Christianity gradually arriving and developing their missions in the Caribbean. The Quakers, for example, had been in Barbados since 1671, and George Fox urged all members of the Society of Friends to treat slaves in a humane manner and to set them free after a certain period of time. In 1754 the Moravians were somewhat surprisingly invited by two wealthy plantation-owners to send missionaries to their estates, and they were the first Christian denomination in Jamaica to attempt in any realistic way the task of teaching Christianity, and its meaning to slaves. It seems fairly clear that, despite their humanity and good intentions, these plantation-owners did not fully understand the real situation vis-a-vis the planters and the slaves, as they were themselves living in England, employing estate managers to run their plantations for them. Planters on the spot were certainly not in favour of anything that gave the negro a sense of his own worth, whether in the eyes of God or of man. Christianity, which might have led to monogamous marriage, was discouraged amongst the slaves. Despite the fact that in 1793 the Consolidated Slave Act had laid down that slaves were to be instructed in religion and baptism by their owners, the law was not widely observed.

After the Moravians, missionaries of other denominations, including Wesleyan Methodists, Baptists, Presbyterians and Congregationalists, quickly followed. The Wesleyan Missionary Society was founded in Jamaica in 1789, and its members were amongst some of the most enthusiastic in their desire to convert the Negro slaves, and also to improve their physical condition and material environment; and they quickly succeeded in arousing the anger and opposition of the planters.

In 1782 there arrived on the Jamaican scene two American negro slaves, George Lisle and Moses Baker, who initiated the Native Baptist Movement. The Baptist denomination has always been the breeding-ground of vastly different and varying levels of thought, belief and faith, and it has embraced all types of disciple – from the scholar, the intellectual and the keen biblical critic to the fundamentalist and literalist, the evangelist and the authoritarian. The two American slaves were simple and uneducated negroes who easily mingled Christian elements of their faith with the superstition and more pagan ideas and ritual of primitive cultures. Before long an invitation was extended by the Government to the Baptist Missionary Society in England to send some of their missionaries to Jamaica. Not unnaturally many slaves were becoming confused concerning the essential message of Christianity, and these missionaries were invited to go in order to establish precisely what the Baptist message was, and to assist in the development of the Baptist mission. The Baptist Missionary Society complied, and the Jamaican Baptist Mission was established in 1814. In 1824 the Presbyterian Church of Jamaica was founded, and the Congregationalists followed soon after.

Despite the sometimes confusing desire to convert to a particular sect or denomination, it should be noted that the nonconformist groups in Jamaica, in general, worked together to protect slaves from excessive cruelty and to improve their condition by providing them with instruction on the sanctity of human life and personality, the importance of self-respect and the development of a sense of individual responsibility. It did not take long for many of the planters to see in all this 'Christianization' a threat to end slavery and, at the same time, their own economic interests – if not their personal safety. The hostility which the planters very clearly expressed soon turned to open threats, and when the threats were ignored there followed deliberate and unveiled persecution. Some groups of proselytizers decided to act with discretion and to compromise; others, however, including the Baptists, stood firm and began to organize a plan for the abolition of slavery and all its attendant evils.

Warning notes were sounded from time to time in the West Indies, and Mrs Carmichael, who spent the years 1821-25 in St Vincent and Trinidad, made it abundantly clear that many mistakes were being made both by the established Church and by nonconformist missionaries. She felt that the Church of England was doing nothing towards the regular religious instruction of slaves, but that in attempting to rectify the situation the zeal of the dissenters had 'far exceeded their prudence'. She attacked, in particular, the Methodists who, according to her, insisted far more upon the sins of 'vain amusements and dress' than upon lying, theft, fighting, cruelty and slander. She went on to present a picture of most missionaries as being both uncultured and uneducated, and consequently unable to enter into some of the refinements of the 'civilized' society of the planters or to raise the social levels of the slaves. She herself saw little wrong with the dances of the negroes which were, in her view, always conducted with great ceremony and propriety. She added that:

> Judging by the conduct of those Negroes who were the most regular attendants at the Methodist chapel, I am unwillingly driven to the belief that the Methodist missions have done little for the cause of true religion, and have rather helped to foster dangerous delusion. The Methodists I fear have done harm; for they have diffused a general feeling among the Negro population that abstaining from dancing, from drinking (a vice, by the way, which Negroes are rarely prone to) and a certain phraseology, which is mere form on their part, is Christianity.

This reaction may have been bias on Mrs Carmichael's part but, in consequence, she set about giving her slaves what she considered to be correct and adequate religious and moral instruction.

If the Methodists taught a somewhat strict code of dress, speech and social behaviour in St Vincent, the Baptists in Jamaica were inculcating a belief in liberty. The Baptists developed a Church membership which was supported by what was known as a 'Baptist ticket'. These 'tickets' were in fact printed cards issued each month to every member of the Baptist congregations by which offerings and weekly attendance were recorded. In addition, they served as passes to church meetings which were regarded as private, and at which on occasion plans for emancipation might be discussed. In fact, the liberty which the Baptists and the Moravians in particular preached was blamed for the slave revolts which broke out in December 1831, and which led to a full-scale Slave Rebellion in 1832, frequently referred to as the 'Baptist War'.

Certainly these two sects were violently attacked by the Established Anglican Church for their responsibility for the affair, and some of their members were very badly treated. A union, called the Colonial Church Union, was founded ostensibly to protect the rights of the Anglican Church, but actually was a somewhat thinly disguised subterfuge designed to destroy the nonconformist missionary effort, to persecute nonconformist supporters and to protect the interests of slave-owners. There followed a vigorous destruction of Baptist, Moravian and Wesleyan chapels, mission-huts and property generally. All this – including the hounding, persecution and beating of the missionaries themselves – was carried out largely by the planters' tough employees. Leaders of the Moravian and Baptist missionary societies, such as H.G. Pfeiffer, William Knibb and Thomas Burchell were arrested and charged with inciting the slave revolt. There can be little doubt that these, and many other nonconformist leaders, had encouraged slaves to put forward demands for improved conditions and ultimate emancipation.

The hundreds of 'Baptist tickets' discovered on the estates where rebels were found were certainly not all planted, but although they were a fair indication of the Baptist support for the ultimate emancipation they hardly constituted proof of any conspiracy or incitement to rebellion by any leaders named. Eventually the missionaries were acquitted and released, and the Government, realizing that both the newly formed Colonial Church Union and the sentiments which inspired it were running counter to the tide of events, wisely disbanded the Union by Royal Proclamation.

After the full emancipation of the slaves in Jamaica on 1 August, 1834, many of the Christian churches, in a much more united effort than they had previously achieved, assisted the released slaves to make the difficult transition from servitude to freedom. The missionaries in particular saw it as a part of their duty to help the new citizens of the colony to purchase plots of land, as well as small dwellings, to enable them to settle down as full members of their society. Throughout the period of transition the Established Church still tended to remain somewhat aloof, in part because it chiefly represented the interests of the planters, who had everything to lose from the increasing self-sufficiency of a liberated slave population, but also because the representatives of the Anglican Church in Jamaica found it very difficult to collaborate with missionaries and denominations which, not so very long before, they had violently persecuted and sought to destroy; or to treat as equals coloured peoples whom they had persistently exhorted to obey their masters and to be content with their condition.

After emancipation and the end of the unsuccessful apprenticeship scheme in 1838 increasing dissatisfaction was expressed with the way in which former slaves and people of the lower classes were being treated. In 1865, Dr Underhill, a Baptist minister, wrote a letter to the Secretary of State for the Colonies in which he described in some detail the living and working conditions in Jamaica which he had observed while living in the island. He complained in particular about the treatment which the lower classes received at the hands of planters and employers generally, and he urged certain reforms. His complaints and assertions were denied by nearly all the *custodes* and the Anglican clergy in Jamaica, but a copy of the letter found its way into the Jamaican newspapers.

In consequence of this, meetings were held in many different towns. Some of the meetings were presided over by George William Gordon, a member of the House of Assembly, supported by a political and religious agitator called Paul Bogle who certainly went much further than Gordon ever intended to go. The Morant Bay Rebellion of 1865 resulted, and – although Gordon was almost certainly innocent – the two men were hanged. The Governor, Mr Edward John Eyre, was subsequently recalled and dismissed from the Imperial Service. The existing Government of Jamaica was forced to resign, the constitution was surrendered, and a Crown Colony government was established. The new Governor, Sir John Peter Grant, disestablished the Church of England, making the Anglican Church just another Christian denomination.

On emancipation there were considerable differences in the religious systems of masters and slaves as a result of the reluctance of slave masters to allow their slaves to be instructed in the Christian faith. In addition, since marriage was established as a religious sacrament, any refusal to allow slaves to become involved in the Christian religion also involved a virtual prohibition of marriages between them. This resulted in a familial disorganization of the slave population; and any existing slave family units were dissolved through the transfer and sale of individual members.

It is not surprising that the refusal to recognise slaves, even after their emancipation, as being worthy of participating fully in Christianity – and all that this implied socially – at the same level as whites resulted in the persistence and development of *a* variety of African cults, which exist even today. It resulted also in attitudes to concubinage and promiscuity which are more often condemned than understood by societies where the Christian ideal of marriage is established. These were attitudes and behavioural forms into which slaves were forced by their masters' own patterns of behaviour, and in which they were deliberately encouraged. Moreover, any innocent tyro reading, or being introduced to, the Old Testament for the first time might possibly be forgiven for believing that the Lord Jehovah himself had sanctioned such activity. Concubines and limited promiscuity were certainly not exactly novel among the ancient Israelites!

Chapter 8
African Survivals

Obeah

It was mentioned in Chapter Five that *obayi*, or the practice of witchcraft, was taken to Jamaica by the African slaves, and that it became their esoteric possession, which they could not share with their white masters and overseers, but which they could, nevertheless, use for their own advantage against their owners and their enemies. Certainly under the conditions of slavery the African negro was virtually forbidden to practise or to perpetuate his own religious culture – stigmatized as pagan.

The more orthodox priestly practice of the Ashanti *okomfo* was as much condemned and forbidden as the blacker arts of the *obayifo*, the witch mainly concerned with antisocial magic. Under conditions of total suppression, where there is literally no escape from the complete control of human life and destiny, it is frequently the less desirable elements that survive and are preserved despite all opposition. The manipulative and esoteric art of the *obayifo* belonged to the realm of the occult, the secret and the hidden even in his own native Ashanti environment. Whilst it has been comparatively easy to forbid and to restrict the common culture of the masses, it has never been found possible to eliminate the gnosis of the elite. This has proved to be true of masonic orders, occult groups, the Dead Sea Sect, the mystery cults or the intelligentsia in Russia.

The white man, in the pursuance of his relentless exploitation and greed for gain, did his utmost to destroy and to negate even the best in African culture, always supporting his arguments the while by illustrations of the worst survivals. Moreover, as the early laws relating to slaves forbade any form of religious assembly whatsoever this inevitably had the effect of encouraging individual and undiscoverable face-to-face relationships with the *obayifo*. Thus obeah became an established practice in Jamaica from the earliest days of slavery, and the obeah-man, or obeah-woman, became a powerful individual within any slave group or community. Witchcraft is an art that is esoterically taught, and the obeah-man who came to Jamaica from Africa ensured that his skills were preserved by training younger men and women to carry on when he had gone.

Obeah is essentially a magical means whereby an individual may obtain his personal desires, eradicate ill-health, procure good fortune in life and business, turn the affections of the objects of his love or lust towards himself, evince retribution or revenge upon his enemies, and generally manipulate the spiritual forces of the cosmos in order to obtain his will. It is the specific function of the obeah-man to provide what his customer desires; for obeah is concerned with the individual and his appetite as opposed to the total good and welfare of the group, tribe or society.

Whilst negroes know who the obeah-men are, it has always been very difficult for white people to discover them. Mrs Carmichael gave evidence of obeah during the early nineteenth century in the Caribbean and suggested that its practice was fatal to negroes, claiming that there was one instance where, in the course of a few months, at least fifteen people died from no other discoverable cause. The negroes so firmly believed in obeah that they hung bottles around their houses, and also in the grounds. These bottles were filled with some infusion specially prepared in order to counteract the evil effects of obeah. They also wore charms or amulets to ward off the malignant obeah power. When, however, a person felt that he was the object of the attentions of an obeah-man, he would say resignedly 'I'm obeahed – I know I'll go dead'.

In the history of the slaves' fight for freedom in Jamaica there are numerous accounts of the use of obeah in order to defeat and to defy the white man. In 1760, for example, there was a slave called Tacky, a Koromantyn who claimed that he had been an African chief and that he had obtained the assistance of the obeah-man in battle. Tacky himself was invested with the further power of catching any shots which were fired at him and of returning them to his opponents. The obeah-men themselves held that they were immune to injury and even to death on the battlefield.

Not only did obeah-men encourage and assist in such slave revolts, but they have also claimed occasionally to be able to raise people from the dead. This may well be a link with the voodoo of the African slaves – mainly Ewe-speaking negroes – who went to Haiti from Whydah and Dahomey. Although voodoo was never fully practised in Jamaica, or in the British West Indies generally, there are certain practices which voodoo and obeah have in common, especially in the areas concerned with death, duppies or jumbies and zombies.

There are two categories of obeah – African and literary – which both reinforce and compete with each other. Many of the magical rites of obeah are extracted from such esoteric literature as *The*

Black Arts, and *The Sixth and Seventh Books of Moses,* which outline techniques of magic quite diverse from the practices of African negroes. On the other hand, the specifically African elements in obeah are concerned in the main with the use of animal and herbal substances, and with the casting of spells in African dialects.

The individuals who became involved in obeah appear in the main to have been people maladjusted to their situation in society or within their family. Obeah provided a common method of discharging tension, if physical violence had been ruled out. The obeah-man often acted as a sorcerer and as a preparer of poisons when his fellow slaves requested this of him. Obeah still seems to permeate the whole social scale in Jamaica, although it is strongly condemned in public, and its practice is a serious criminal offence. Under the Victorian Acts of 1840, 1856 and 1857 it became clear that obeah was considered a potent and dangerously antisocial activity. Even a consultation with an obeah-man was punishable with hard labour to a maximum of three months, whilst any individual convicted by a criminal court for practising obeah might receive twelve months with hard labour and seventy-eight lashes of the whip.

But although forbidden by law, obeah is still firmly believed in and practised by a large number of people throughout Jamaica. The hanging up of obeah bottles and bags is quite common in the rural areas and in yard communities, and is certainly not unknown in urban districts. One recent Jamaican informant, a native of Clarendon, insisted that three quarters of the population in his own village believed in obeah and other forms of witchcraft, and that those who were able availed themselves of it. According to him all the older generation accepted obeah as a fact, whilst the less intelligent of the younger generation were influenced by it. He claimed that a really rich man – and sometimes just a very desperate man – would pay fifty or more English pounds in order to obtain cures for his ailments, to discover the person responsible for the death of another, or to settle problems or family quarrels. He knew obeah-men who lived in the hills outside the village; they themselves did not go into the village, but people went to see them by special appointment, usually during the hours of darkness, and anonymously.

There is naturally a great deal of suspicion expressed towards people enquiring into the extent of obeah and its reality. Nevertheless, it is indisputable that not only does obeah persist within the

Jamaican community, but also the obeah-man is a powerful consultant on a great variety of matters including a child's education.

There are something like thirty or more terms in current use which are synonymous with, or euphemisms for, the obeah-man, such as balm-man, bush-doctor, do-good man, professor, four-eyed man, buzu man, guzu man, zuzu man, jumby man, shadow-catcher and knife-and-scissors man. At all costs one must keep the real nature of the obeah-man secret. He keeps his 'things' in his *obi* place; his *bush* is a concoction in which medicinal or poisonous herbs are essential ingredients. Without his *bush* he is lost and power-less; in fact, his strength, power or force is his *guzu*. Since he is a scientific man, and his magic is in reality another form of *science,* he becomes a 'professor' or 'knife-and-scissors man'. Today in Jamaica a distinction is made between obeah, which is prohibited by law, and balmyards and faithhealing, which are quite legal.

People's beliefs travel with them: they are inseparable. Obeah is part and parcel of Jamaican and British West Indian culture. It is, therefore, inevitable that Jamaicans, or some of them at least, living in Britain should retain their inherited beliefs. A social worker in mental health in South London has recently stated that one of the greatest problems experienced by West Indians in our complex society is not merely the clash of culture, but the persistence of the belief in and fear of obeah. She described in some detail the great anxiety of one Jamaican woman who had been 'obeahed', and who could not be treated by any usual techniques. Her only 'cure' ultimately was to have a bath in which a copper coin had been placed.

Duppies and the Anancy-Tacooma Folk Cycle

Strongly linked with the practice of obeah is the belief in and fear of ghosts or duppies. The Jamaican word duppy (duppie or duppe) derives from the Bube word *dupe*, meaning a ghost. Originally, among the Ashanti, there was a very clear distinction made between the *saman* and the *sasa* elements in the human being. The *saman* was the ghost, apparition or spectre which was the form in which the dead sometimes become visible upon earth. On the other hand, the *sasa* was the invisible spiritual power of an individual which disturbed the mind of the living, or worked a spell upon them so that they might suffer in a variety of ways. It was, in fact, that part of the person which had to be 'laid' or rendered harmless at the funeral ceremony. The *saman* was originally the equivalent of the *duppy,* whilst the *sasa* was the shadow of the individual. In modern Jamaica both terms would certainly be covered by the one word duppy. Other equivalents of duppy are *bugaboo* and *jumby*, although the latter (in a variety of forms) is generally used exclusively of an evil spirit or ghost.

The duppy is frequently blamed for things that are evil or go wrong in modern Jamaican society. Indeed, duppies have been known to make the headlines in the current national press – but so, of course, have poltergeists in England. Duppies can work through people, animals, birds and plants, and in fact any bird associated with duppies by popular superstition is referred to as a 'duppy bird'. And just as elves are associated with toadstools so duppies are closely linked with mushrooms, which are still referred to as 'duppy caps' and 'duppy umbrellas' in Jamaica. The duppy has an unpredictable character, sometimes helpful, sometimes harmful: now he will assist man, now he will become malicious and revengeful. The *mmoatia* of the Ashanti had the same unpredictability – they removed things, were generally mischievous, threw stones at people; and like the *mmoatia* the duppies live and play around the odum or silk-cotton tree.

A great deal of obeah ritual is concerned with this belief in duppies and the catching of a person's shadow by the 'shadow-catcher' or obeah-man. Because of its persistently antisocial activities obeah gave rise to movements which sought to provide an antidote to its black and evil magic. Obeah is essentially the worship of evil as formerly represented by the Ashanti devil, Sasabonsam – a monster, grotesque and malicious, associated with the woods and in particular, the odum tree, which he uses as a headquarters from which he captivates unwary hunters. In conjunction with the duppies, the chief of demons gives power to the obeah-man's fetishes.

Associated with this belief in duppies and demons is the whole Ananse-Ntikuma folk-tale corpus which was mentioned earlier, in Chapter Five. In the Jamaican stories the name of the spider appears in a variety of ways – Anancy, Annancy, Anansay, Nancy and Ananse. His son, Ntikuma in the Ashanti stories, has become Tacoma, Tecoma, Tackoma, Tacoomah and Tacooma. Anancy stories include beast fables, resembling some of the Ashanti cycle, and fairy tales which are closer to the European tradition.

Anancy is featured as a figure of greed, envy, spite, revenge, deceit, theft and mischief. Cunning is glorified in his activities in which he is sometimes overreached by his son, Tacooma, and assisted by his wife Crookie. He outwits his betters and frequently ignores moral principles. He is at best an amoral figure; at worst he is blatantly immoral; probably his best feature is that he outwits the sheer brute strength of others with his cunning. In general, the character Anancy is used as a portmanteau figure to explain some apparently inexplicable event – not unlike the *asylum ignorantiae* of an 'act of God'. The individual will often be satisfied with the statement, 'Oh, Anancy, he do it!'

One of the characters in the Anancy cycle of stories is Brother Duppy who is represented as a supernatural being; he is the enemy of Brother Anancy yet is also evil in his activities, so at times there is little distinction between their actions. Perhaps it is a reflection of the difficulty that all primitive theologies have in expressing the difference between the functions of God and the Devil, Yahweh and Satan, Ormuzd and Ahriman, Allah and Iblis. Thus at times Brother Anancy may seem a relatively harmless fellow in the context of children's stories, but he then turns out to be as unpredictable as Brother Duppy himself. He is very much the trickster figure of the North American Indian cycles.

It will be remembered that the original Ashanti stories usually began with the statement, 'We do not really mean, we do not really mean that what we are going to say is true', and conclude with the rider, 'This is my story which I have told, and if it be sweet, or if it be not sweet, some you may accept as true and the rest you may praise me for telling it'. The Jamaican Anancy story usually concludes with the formula, 'Jack Mandora, me no choose none'. The origin of 'Jack Mandora' is unknown (Louise Bennett suggests 'Jack the Doorman'); but the phrase as a whole may mean something like 'there is a moral, but it is not pointed at anyone in particular'; or possibly 'there is a moral but I'm not going to particularize it'. Another suggestion is that the word 'Mandora' may be connected with the Spanish-Portuguese word *mentira,* meaning a lie. The teller may originally have had the Ashanti concept in mind – 'Some you may accept as true; some as falsehood; make your own choice'.

Myalism

As opposed to obeah, or black magic, myalism was originally a form of white magic and healing cult, claiming to counteract the evil powers of obeah. The origin of the word is in some doubt, the most likely etymology being F.G. Cassidy's suggestion that it derives from the

Ewe (and Hausa) *maye,* meaning evil, and, *le,* to take hold of, to grasp. Myalism seeks to 'grasp the evil' that is produced by obeah and to destroy it. It was the function of the myal-man to create a stronger magic than that of the obeah-man. There was a specific myal dance by means of which negroes were initiated into the myal society, through a death and resurrection ritual. There seems little doubt that in the early days of slavery many of the myalist rituals took the place of the African *rites de passage* which gave stability and a sense of identity to their society.

Myalism appears to have been the old tribal religion of the Ashanti in which the Supreme Being, Nyame or Nyankonpon was worshipped, and there was also veneration for the minor deities *(abosom)* subordinate to Nyankonpon, who appeared in Jamaica in the guise of Accompong. The priest of myalism openly opposed the obeah-man. The myal-man was, in fact, almost fanatical in his zeal to destroy the works of the evil obeah, and he demanded a fetish oath of allegiance from initiates into his myal society. It was their committed duty to 'dig up the obeah' wherever it might be found.

The initiation ceremonies, the wild possession dance, and the death and resurrection rite supervised by the myal-man, all led up to the suppression of myalism by the white man. It is an interesting reflection that what, in reality, was the less harmful and more positive aspect of Ashanti religion, received the stronger condemnation, and in consequence led to the greater intensification of the more evil forms of practice. It was with the suppression of myalism in Jamaica that obeah began to gain an ascendancy and to become a quasi-religion with intense hatred for the white man, and with the object of the ultimate overthrow of the white masters.

The techniques and rituals of myalism, after its suppression, were quickly adopted and absorbed by the obeah-men, so that they managed to perform the duties of both the priest of myalism and the 'shadow-catcher', often to the extent of digging up their own obeah in order to demonstrate their supreme power. Thus, whereas formerly the obeah-man put obeah upon someone, and the myal-man's function was to 'pull' it, now both functions came within the province of the obeah-man. It is not surprising, therefore, that from then on the white population identified myalism with obeah.

In her interesting and provocative book, *Jamaica: The Search for an Identity,* Katrin Norris has suggested that it is not contradictory to say that Jamaicans have adopted Christianity without abandoning the traditions of African religious ritual. After the establishment of the Wesleyan Missionary Society in Jamaica in 1789, the emotional element in Methodism in particular, appealed to the spirit of myalism among the negroes; so that the long-forbidden rites of the Ashanti were now resuscitated in connexion with the services of the Methodist Church.

Under the aegis of Methodist Revivalism myalism took on a completely fresh lease of life. Christianity was to some extent the veneer which covered what was, in fact, a recrudescence of tribal solidarity still bound by the solemn fetish oath. Similarly, the Native Baptist Churches, which began to develop after the arrival in 1782 of the American negro slaves, George Lisle and Moses Baker, became associations of slaves whose concern it was to mingle the beliefs and rituals of myalism with Christian observances.

After the abolition of slavery there was a very strong resurgence of myalism. These outbreaks occurred with a certain regularity between 1841 and 1860. In 1842 the outbreaks were generally in the areas of Montego Bay, St James, Hanover, Westmoreland and Trelawney. Services were held under cotton trees, sensay fowls were sacrificed, wild songs were sung, and the dancing became increasingly uncontrolled until participants fell to the ground writhing, muttering incoherently, grunting and finally became completely exhausted. And whatever the purpose of the dance might have been, its expression was sensual. This dance was believed by the participants to be the means of reaching identity with their ancestors whose spirits entered them and communicated with them. The more Christian interpretation was that these experiences were of a Pentecostal nature and that the incoherence of the communicants was an expression of the 'gift of tongues'.

As these myalist revivals continued, the individuals involved took on a prophetic function and claimed to have visions; the myal people became 'angel men'. They declared that Christ was coming and that the end of the world was at hand; in the meantime, God had sent them to 'pull' the obeahs and to catch all the shadows that remained spell-bound at the cotton trees. It is true that charges were made for these particular 'services', but the myalists were in two respects abstemious – they neither drank nor smoked. They were, however, a disruptive influence within the Christian churches, interrupting services and using them for the promotion of myalist beliefs. Their words were treasured as divine revelation. The years 1860-61 saw a great religious revival, during which the myalist incursions reached a climax; prayer and fasting mingled freely with 'wild extravagance and almost blasphemous fanaticism', as one contemporary put it.

If Christianity became tainted by myalism in the atmosphere of revivalism, it is equally certain that over the years myalism became something very different from the pristine African cult of the Ashanti of pre-slavery days. Then it was a form of worship of the Supreme Being, part of a negro way of life in an uncontaminated culture. In current revivalist outbreaks it takes a decadent form, and yet it is still able, as Father J.J. Williams has said in *Voodoos and Obeahs*, to 'vitalize each recurrent upheaval against formal Christianity'.

Chapter 9
Revivalism and Pocomania

Bedwardism

A people who have been freed after many decades of slavery will obviously seek to establish some form of identity as a group. In Jamaica the only real links of the freed slaves were certainly not with the long since defunct Arawaks, nor with the planters, nor yet with the somewhat cautious and theologically forbidding Christian ministers but with their ancestors in Africa, the land of their origin. In the 1860s there spread through Jamaica a movement which attempted to restore and revitalize their natural spiritual inheritance. This movement was called 'The Great Revival' and 'The Great Awakening', and it developed into what must, at times, have been a frightening return to mass trance states, abandoned dancing, sexual excitement and orgies, public confessions, masochistic forms of self-punishment and flagellation. This sort of 'revivalist' movement was as sporadic as it was spontaneous: it lacked organisation and direction as well as a real, critical understanding of its own purpose. Like many other popular movements directed at, and by, ignorant people it depended very much upon the persuasion and eloquence of the few.

We have already seen how myalism developed out of the desire for self-expression and self-fulfilment through some recollection and recreation of the African past. But the decay of myalism as a separate and identifiable religious force was inevitable, and it would probably have disappeared altogether but for the new scope for its spirit and traditional ritual discovered in Methodism and among the so-called Native Baptist Congregation. A people who have recently acquired freedom after a long period of cruel repression often look for some temporary messiah who might at least give them some spiritual solace and a sense of divine or supernatural redemption.

Such a man was Alexander Bedward (b. 1859) who, in 1894, established the Jamaica Baptist Church in August Town, St Andrew, and became its leader or Shepherd. Bedward claimed that he received visions from God himself, and that in him many of the prophets such as Jonah, Moses and John the Baptist, were reincarnated. Writing in 1916, Father A.J. Emerick held that Bedwardism had all the hallmarks of mysticism, and that it had fundamentally the same origin. Bedward believed that the Spirit of God had descended upon him, and had revealed to him that the waters of the Hope River would cleanse from all sin, all evil and all diseases. Every Wednesday morning as many as twenty or thirty thousand negroes are reported to have gathered by the river near August Town. There Bedward appeared in his regalia, a resplendent white robe, holding a magical wand in his hand. Before healings took place there was a series of elaborate ceremonies and a ritual blessing of the water. Many hundreds of 'cures' were claimed as a result of the dipping of individuals in the River Hope.

There were, however, many among the Jamaican people who were not impressed by Bedward's achievements, and they composed a mocking popular song about his activities:

Dip dem, Bedward, dip dem;
Dip dem in de healing stream;
Some come from de Eas',
Dem favour wil' beas'.
Dip dem in de healing stream;
Dip dem, Bedward, dip dem;
Dip dem in de healing stream.

Bedward has been referred to as a 'religious monomaniac', but there is evidence to suggest that he was something other than this. It is true that he did some rather mad things; in 1920 he proclaimed himself the Messiah, or Christ, the Son of God. This was no mean claim by a man who was virtually illiterate and a labourer; though no doubt his many followers felt that he compared quite favourably with one who, making similar claims, was in fact the son of a carpenter's wife. Bedward was formerly a member of the Methodist Church; however, he possessed just that element of eloquence and persuasion which impressed a profoundly inarticulate group who, because of their frustration and desperation, barely noticed the blasphemy in Bedward's claim. Many of them were, in any case, used to missionaries who preached of Christ's Second Coming at almost any moment in time, and anyone who seemed to fulfil these prophecies and all that they implied was welcomed.

No doubt Bedward received considerable support from certain elements in his society who were looking for a leader and a prophet. There may have been much confusion in Bedward's own mind as to his exact role – now he was Christ, now he was the Baptist, now he was Elijah – but it mattered little so long as his followers saw in him something of a supernatural order. Soon, like Elijah, he prophesied that he would be taken up into heaven; after this he would return in power to the earth and would gather together his elect. After his 'Second Coming' the earth would be destroyed in a cataclysmic and apocalyptic convulsion, involving hurricanes, fires, earthquakes and general devastation.

Like many other religious leaders in man's history Bedward went too far. In an unguarded moment he stated that his 'ascension' would take place on 31 December, 1920. The day approached and then passed; Bedward failed to fulfil this – the ultimate in prophecies. Then, like all prophets who have over-reached themselves by being too precise, Bedward attempted to quieten his followers by further predictions. Eventually, after a whole series of failures, Bedward was arrested and confined in a mental home. There is, however, a strong suspicion that Bedward's confinement was partly politically motivated and since his preaching was strongly political he represented a danger to the status quo.

There is always an element of tragedy in the charismatic leader who lacks the power to fulfil his promise, and the history of religious revival and messianism is replete with sorrowful stories of leaders retiring to homes for the mentally unbalanced or, perhaps more cynically, to their own mansions where they may practise a comfortable and 'divinely sanctioned' polygamy; or who like the Mahdi or Bab end their days in violence or ignominy. Perhaps even more sad is the fact that thousands of Bedward's followers who came from all over the island of Jamaica, having sold all their possessions however few they might have been, had waited with Bedward to ascend with him into heaven as God's Elect. Thus his failure was theirs as well. Yet, this was by no means the end of Bedwardism, for his church in August Town still exists to commemorate his life and memory; and Bedwardites are still in the official list of religious sects.

Pocomania

It is not easy to see where myalism, revivalism, Bedwardism, Zionism or Pocomania begin and end. They have all obviously borrowed from one another, as well as from the great variety of Christian sects and denominations that have developed in Jamaica. They all owed much to the general feeling of frustration and depression that resulted from the treatment of the people after the Morant Bay Rebellion. People who are prevented from one form of expression quickly find solace in another.

The origin of the word 'Pocomania' is itself obscure. Writing in

1929 Martha Beckwith, in her *Black Roadways,* stated that the revivalist and the obeah-man united in the 'particular religious cult known as Pukkumerian'. Beckwith held that the Pukkumerians regarded the term as a derisory one applied to them by their enemies, and she considered that they were simply revivalist like the rest. She also offered 'pick them here' as a possible etymology, meaning 'dig here for the buried obeah' and referring to the function of the Pocomanians in opposing the black obeah with white magic. She went on to describe how they held their meetings near graveyards, and appealed to the ghosts of their own members when they summoned spirits to a meeting. Members of the cult would dance, jump and sing, and they spoke in a secret language understood by the spirits.

Attempts at an etymology are probably more inspired by the described activities of the religious participants than by accurate philological research. The Twi word *po* means 'to shake or tremble', *kom* means 'to dance in a wild state of frenzy', and to these two elements it is possible that *myal* has been added, thus making a cult which mingles revivalism with ancestor spirit-possession. Another suggestion is that the word has a Spanish origin, *poco* meaning 'little', plus mania or madness. This is not impossible and might well be used derogatively, in the manner suggested by Martha Beckwith, by the enemies of Pocomania, implying that the practitioners were a little mad. Others relate the word to the Kimbundu *kumona,* meaning 'to see', implying that under possession by the ancestral spirits the participants are endowed with the power to see the world of the occult, and to have paranormal experiences. Finally, it has been suggested that Poco dancing derived from the indentured Indians who came to Jamaica to help solve the labour problems after the emancipation of slaves, and that the word *poco* is a corruption of the Hindi *pukka,* meaning 'real'. The devotees of Pocomania in fact suffered from a real *mania,* such as that experienced by dancing dervishes.

Pocomania began in the 1920s and in general terms was a revival of the magical beliefs and trance techniques of African religion blended, at the more emotional and ecstatic levels, with Christianity. Professor F. Henriques traces its origin back to the myal movement of the slaves which was directed against the obeah-men. Despite the condemnation of Pocomania by both the middle and upper classes, who see in it a lowering of the general tone of their society, it is not really practised in secret. Social distance may have quite opposite effects upon a group of people; some may elide that distance by a pretence that differences do not exist, and so glaring oppositions may be hidden; others may seek to emphasize those differences by giving them a ritual form in order fully to establish their group identity. The devotees of Pocomania are concerned with social identification, and with combating the evil forces of obeah. Their methods, however, are really the equivalent of the production of a white magic effectively to destroy a black magic, in a way similar to that in which myalism itself initially attempted to oppose obeah.

Those who practise Pocomania hold their services either in special meeting halls, huts or in yards in the open air, called poco-yards. They usually begin their services by singing revivalist hymns, accompanied by clapping and stamping, and they frequently continue their activities far into the night. The purpose of the singing and physical activity is to produce a rhythm which, in turn, will result in a trance state. In this state various psychic phenomena take place, and the devotees believe that they are taken over by spirits who speak through them and talk in a variety of 'tongues'. There is thus a combination of spiritualistic medium activities and the glossolalia, or speaking with tongues, which the disciples experienced at Pentecost. Worshippers are convinced that they are being guided by entities referred to as 'Captain', 'Mother' or 'Shepherd', or possibly by a plurality of 'captains' and so forth. This whole experience has a great deal in common with the practice of voodoo in Haiti, in which the *loa,* or 'divine horsemen', possess the worshippers and ride them to a final state of prostration. Pocomanians are also known to use herbs and drugs in order to induce the trance state in which eventually the spirits take possession.

The Pocomanians follow most of the usages of the revivalists: for example, a meeting-place in the open-air may be little more than a circle marked on the ground, with a rough table in the centre covered by a white cloth. Under the table there are lighted candles whose function is to attract spirits emerging from mysterious-looking bottles. The ground is frequently marked out in a specific way inside a circle some thirty-six feet in diameter – beyond which is 'the world'. In the centre there are three concentric circles, in which there is placed a triangular stone referred to as the 'power key'. These three circles represent God the Father, God the Son and God the Holy Spirit. Around the triangular stone there will usually be candles, fruits and flowers, whilst upon the stone itself a chicken will be sacrificed and the 'power key' will be covered with its blood – reminiscent of the sacrifice of both the Ancient Hebrews and the Africans.

This stone is the control point through which all the spiritual powers will enter into the circle and make their presence felt. In addition to the experience of possession it is claimed that miraculous cures take place, particularly through baptisms and washings at sacred pools in the yards. The sick are frequently washed in holy water which may be contained in a bottle. This washing reflects more the 'soul-washing' of African tradition than the baptism of the Christian church. Thus the leader of the Pocomanian group is regarded as a worker of miracles, particularly of healing; he is a thaumaturge and Pocomania is thaumaturgical.

The opponents and critics of Pocomania have repeatedly attacked it as a form of devil worship, and its followers have been referred to as 'Black Israelites'. It appears that Pocomanians invoke fallen angels, including the Prince of Darkness himself, under the title Lucifer. Some of their ritual appears to many to be little more than a caricature of Christian ritual. There is, for example, a reflection of the Eucharist or Lord's Supper in the Pocomanian ceremony at the close of the first part of the service, when food and drink are offered to all in attendance, and the altar is then smashed. In some meetings the arrangement of candles, flowers and fruits is kicked around the circle, and often the fruit is thrown in a hostile way into the audience.

Generally speaking, the devotees of Pocomania do not use musical instruments, except perhaps a small drum, to arouse their dancing and singing fervour. In order to 'get the spirit' the participants develop a technique of breathing heavily and rhythmically until the trance state is induced. Ganja and rum are also used to disorient consciousness and make the individual more susceptible to possession. This technique, in which the person breathes with a short, sharp intake, is sometimes referred to as 'trooping' or 'trumping'. In prayer the Pocomanians have a ritual of 'Calling Sixty', which is an attempt to speak with the spirits who ruled during the Revivalist period of the 1860s.

A comparison of the numbers and percentages of followers of Pocomania in 1843 and 1960 indicates a falling-off from 0.3 per cent to 0.05 per cent of the total population; in round figures this represents a fall from something like 4,000 adherents to a mere 800. But this seriously underrates its actual strength, since many Pocomanians are quite unwilling to admit that they support Pocomania as a cult, or that they are in any way connected with it. Many of them are, in fact, concurrently members of one of the more orthodox churches, so that an accurate estimate of Pocomanian followers is quite impossible. It is also true that many of the American Revivalist cults resemble very closely the sort of enthusiasm and fanaticism of Pocomania, and are able to provide most of what the Pocomanians seek.

Without suggesting any historical or etymological link between the two, it is very interesting from a comparative point of view to look at the religion of the Pokomo who live on Mafia Island off the coast of Tanzania. The population of the island is Muslim and the Pokomo are lowest in the status ladder, largely because they are racially least Arabian and most African. In consequence, they find themselves excluded from the tribal life of the island as well as from political participation. But, in addition, they find no place in the religious and ritual life of the island society. Like so many other subject and depressed peoples, they have sought to find fulfilment in a cult of spirit possession, and in and through this cult they have developed an influence and power in the total community. This 'possession syndrome' is an attempt to find a 'self which can provide power, which is beyond question or challenge during the period of possession and which the world has refused to allow the individual, in normal life. This position with regard to members of depressed groups has no better expression than the comment of Sheila Patterson in her *Dark Strangers*:

> The cults focus the attention of their members on another world, a world of spirits and magic in which the initiated are no longer underprivileged. All members can share in the satisfaction of being a part of an elite in relation to the rest of the world, while the many leaders and office-holders, all drawn from more or less the same sphere as the ordinary members, gain an additional semi-messianic satisfaction which is denied them in everyday life. And while the close-knit cult groups give their members a feeling of belonging to an elect community they also provide entertainment, sensuous thrills, and emotional release to people living out a drab, poverty-stricken, and hopeless existence.

Zionism and Other Forms of Revivalism

The Zion cult is another revivalist cult similar in many respects to Pocomania itself. It involves the same sort of ritual dancing leading to collective possession by the archaic African deities (abosom) as well as by such biblical characters as the archangels, Michael and Gabriel, the prophets Samuel and Jeremiah, and a strange mixture of other personalities such as Jehovah, the Holy Ghost, Moses, Solomon, Rachel, Miriam, Jesus Christ and even Satan. The Old Testament is invariably more in evidence in their knowledge and ritual than the New Testament. The rite of baptism is practised by some Zion cults as a sort of *rite de passage* similar to African initiation ceremonies.

Not all sects that carry the name 'Zion' in their title are necessarily connected with the Zion Revivalist movement, although most attempt to conventionalize and make respectable something that has never received general approval or acceptance. The author recalls a visit he made to a small Zionist church at Annotto Bay, which had the unlikely name of the Mt Olivet African Episcopal Zion Church. It was situated in a rambling yard, an area which clearly served as a balm-yard, if not a poco-yard. The church itself was a small hut, part of which was used as a nursery school for the yard community. There was a special altar area which housed dozens of bottles filled with water blessed by the 'bishop' of the church, who apparently had come over from America specially to perform the ceremony. Each bottle had the name of a church member written on it and the intention was that the water could be used for drinking, anointing or bathing if the member was sick. The church had its balm-woman, who preferred to be called 'minister' and to be addressed with the orthodox title of 'reverend'. She was neatly dressed in a well-cut costume and matching hat, but she was, for all her apparent sophistication compared with the members of the Yard community, a balm-woman who believed in and displayed her powers of healing to the common people.

Writing in 1965, Vittorio Lanternari suggested that both Pocomania and the Zion Revival Movement were replete with African traditional and pagan rituals which religious leaders in Jamaica exploited to arouse the protests of the black people against cultural and religious domination by the white man. Certainly there is some truth in this. For a very long time traditional Christian religion was controlled by white priests and missionaries, and many of the revivalist cults were an expression of protest against white domination, whilst the recrudescence of African rituals indicated an attempt to claim something which was specifically non-European.

In its singing and dancing rituals Zionism uses small kettle-drums, from nine to twelve inches in diameter, and possibly a base drum, about two feet in diameter. In addition, metal triangles, tambourines and 'shakers', usually made from dried calabash gourds (*shakas*) which hold pebbles and are fixed to a stick handle, are used. Participants in the ritual form a circle, from the centre of which a leader will direct the 'drilling' and groaning, the intake of breath once more – as in Pocomania – being used as a rhythmic instrument. Eventually the whole group will be dancing under the possession of the archaic ancestors, a process usually referred to as 'jumping'.

Whilst under the influence of this spirit possession the Revivalist receives inspiration and 'teachment', which he passes on to the group. Sometimes he becomes 'two-minded' or confused, not knowing whether the words he speaks are 'god-inspired' or represent his own mistaken ideas. In nearly all the revivalist groups the leaders and sub-leaders are referred to as 'Shepherds' or 'Captains'; in some instances the highest rank is that of 'Father'. Such high office may be reached by a crowned shepherd who has served for some considerable time, and is highly respected by his own and other groups.

The subordinate shepherds have a variety of functions. One may be a 'wheeling' shepherd who dances round and round the ritual table like a Muslim dervish, sometimes performing conjuring tricks, or juggling with glasses filled with water or balancing them upon his head. Another may be a 'warrior' shepherd, sometimes referred to as a 'captain', whose function it is to protect the ceremonial and ritual area from alien, intrusive influences. The function of the 'hunting' shepherd is similar in that he must hunt out every corner of the yard area, meeting all spirits that have entered, both good and bad, and registering their presence.

Another shepherd seeks to divine the future with the aid of the spiritual entities present, and he has the title of 'rambling' shepherd. All these shepherds work together, the 'warrior' shepherd seeking to protect the area, the 'hunting' shepherd recognizing the evil spirits present, and finally a 'cutting' shepherd whose main function it is to cut out of the area any evil influences that have managed to evade the careful policing of the other shepherds.

Women also have specific functions in the revivalist sect, sometimes equivalent to those of the men. There is often a 'Mother', who is the highest female officer, frequently referred to as the 'Shepherdess'. Sometimes the female leader is called the 'Queen-dove', and it is her function to coo like a dove during the revivalist ceremonies. She may be a 'Bible-pointer', in which office she will read out the Bible text which the preacher wishes to expound – she *points* the subject of the sermon. There are some revivalist groups which are essentially matriarchal, and in which the female leader has male shepherds as her assistants and subordinates.

One of the interesting features of most of these revivalist meetings is the enjoyment which the participants derive from giving their testimonies, during which each individual will lay his soul bare and tell the story of his life, including all his peccadilloes as well as his greater sins. There is virtually a competition to see who can provide the most amusing, or the most shocking life-story. This 'soul-washing', or spiritual strip-tease resembles in many respects the 'sharing' sessions of the Buchmanites.

Through participation in the practices of the revivalist groups, in singing, dancing, groaning, spirit possession, giving of testimonies and the rituals and *rites de passage,* including baptism, anointing and communion, and the sense of identity of all 'within the circle' and exclusion of all outside, the members obtain that self-fulfilment and social satisfaction which Jamaican life in general has failed to give them. Their colour is forgotten or idealized, their poverty transcended, and their isolation overcome through communion with a spirit in which they find identity with the past, the present and the future via their ever-present ancestors. The problems of politics, society, culture and economics disappear before the all-pervasive presence, not of the Divine, but of the host of spiritual witnesses to their racial integrity.

Chapter 10
Cumina and Other Ceremonies

Cumina

The word *cumina* (with its many variants, such as *kumina, kumona, krumuna, koominah, cummona, crumuna*) is of doubtful origin. Cassidy and Page suggest that two or more words of related meaning are probably combined. The Twi word *kom* connotes 'to dance wildly in a state of frenzy or ecstasy ascribed by the natives to the agency of a fetish, *nkom-moa*, spirit of possession'. The Kimbundu word *kumona* means to see in a sort of clairvoyant way through possession, possibly by some ancestor spirit.

The cumina, then, was most likely originally an African ceremonial dance held as a memorial for the departed, in which members of the tribe, individually and collectively, felt that they were literally possessed by their ancestors and that they established through their somewhat phrenetic dancing an identity with the ghosts of the dead. The solidarity of the group or tribe was thus perpetually maintained.

There is another African cult word also in use in Jamaica, namely, *cumama* which has reference to 'calling dead mother'. Although this is not related etymologically to *cumina* it, nevertheless, refers to a similar ritual in which the spirits of the dead are invoked. It is just possible that there is some connexion between the Jamaican practice and some of the ceremonies of the aboriginal Arawak Indians, for apparently *cumana* is a term found in the Arawak Venezuelan region of South America.

The earliest references to the ceremony of Cumina in Jamaica are found in 1943 in which a native dance of some sort is implied. The cult is highly localized, occurring mainly in the parish of St Thomas and in Kingston, primarily among people claiming descent from, or affinity with, the Maroons of the Blue Mountains. The Jamaicans themselves regard it as an African cultural survival; and, to quote from the publicity for the Tivoli Gardens Kumina Group in 1971, 'it consists of some of the most exciting drumming, singing and dancing to be found in all Jamaican Folk Music'.

There are two views about the nature and function of Cumina. One is that it is purely an art form which is being recreated largely by Jamaican intellectuals, particularly at the University of the West Indies in Kingston. As an art form, developed at the University's Creative Arts Centre Theatre, it is not merely replicating African dance and ceremonial movements, but it is also attempting to provide some sophistication of its elemental form and structure. It is, in short, part of the search for a cultural identity which can be expressed in a vivid, active and creative art form.

A second view is that the Cumina embraces a whole catena of religious beliefs and ceremonies which are much more important than any art form to the average Jamaican. The Cumina represents the recrudescence of certain African *rites de passage* and religious concepts. This does not mean, of course, that it cannot be performed artistically, or even in some sophisticated form, but that these are simply the unimportant external developments and trimmings of a spiritual reality. The times of birth, betrothal, wake and entombment are periods fraught with danger when the human spirit might be invaded and even destroyed by evil and malicious duppies, unless protected by specially devised ceremonial prayers and dances. By means of these ceremonies the evil powers are held at bay whilst ancestral spirits, gods and guardians are invoked, enter the worshippers and protect them from the awesome dangers that surround them.

The Cumina has its chief or master of ceremonies who is responsible for the whole conduct of the rituals, and in this he is assisted by a Queen or Mother of the Cumina, who is a singer of some competence and is sometimes referred to as 'the black and white girl'. This is because, during the process of the rituals, she frequently wears the badge of office of the master of ceremonies which he passes on to her at certain junctures. This badge is a black and white cord worn around the neck. The Queen herself has a prodigious knowledge of all the folk songs involved in the various ceremonies – songs which all have a peculiar significance for each separate rite.

The gods invoked are the old African tribal gods, such as Macoo, 'who causes a possessed zombie to climb up poles and trees backwards', Kanuba, a spirit who comes from the father, his father and father's father, Kish and many other tribal gods. Among these gods and spirits are zombies, led by the King zombie called Oto; a zombie in this context is an ancestral spirit or god, or a living person who has been possessed by one of these ancestral spirits. Just as the four corners of the earth are guarded by four sky gods, so the four corners of the ceremonial booth are watched over by the four evangelists.

Ceremonies begin with greeting the gods, which is in the nature of an invitation to zombies, gods and spirits to enter the heads of the ceremonial drums. This involves the beating of the rims of the drums with a specific rhythm. When the zombies or gods are at last considered to be present in the drums they are said to be 'hot'. The gods are then welcomed officially and fed, and the ceremonial dance begins. At some ceremonies a goat may be sacrificed as a part of a purificatory rite, and the walls of the booth become lined with ancestral spirits. As the ceremony proceeds the drums are mounted by a succession of drummers each of whom strives, eventually, to play the lead drum.

As the ancestral spirits, or zombies, take possession of the drummers and dancers, the activities become wilder, and extremely difficult physical contortions are performed. Participants clap their hands continually and stamp their feet in an attempt to liven the spirit, whilst they 'beat de hymn' in continuous chorus. During marriage ceremonies the drums are tuned and 'set' in a slightly different manner after they have been invoked and plentifully sprayed with rum.

There is, of course, a revivalist spirit about Cumina but whereas Pocomania and Zion have a more specifically Christian element, the cult of Cumina is basically African and non-Christian. Some of the gods and zombies contacted certainly have Old Testament names, such as Jah, Ezekiel, Uriah and so forth, and the quaternity of gods, guardians or evangelists operates for protective purposes, but essentially the whole proceedings are African in origin. They ask the spirits for economic, social and medical help and for the solution to daily problems, such as the success of the individual in litigation, with a lover or in obtaining a job. Aid is invoked to exorcise evil spirits, and thanks and sacrifice are given for any help received. Rituals may extend as long as a night and a day but rarely longer.

Edward Seaga, in his *Folk Music of Jamaica,* claims to have identified about forty words of Congo origin used in Cumina ritual songs. To be precise, most of the words he mentions are pure San Salvador Kikongo. Songs are classified as *bilah* (or *bailo*) and are couched primarily in English dialect, or in *country,* which is an African dialect taught by spirits only to those who are the vehicles of their possession. Cumina devotees make their *kbandu* drums from small coconut wood kegs; they are headed on one side only with goat-skin which is attached by nails driven through a band which surrounds the drum head. The drums are usually about two feet in length and one foot in diameter; the drummer sits astride his drum which he plays with his hands, using a steady, regular beat. In some of the more complete rites larger drums are also used, and if a particular spirit is being called, charmed or greeted a specific form of drumming is used termed 'playing cast'. In addition to drums *shakas* are used. Cumina devotees also use a percussion instrument referred to as a *kata-tik,* or *catta-stick,* and a grater made from a small tin sheet with nail-punched holes over which a small strip of metal is scraped to a rhythm.

Thus Cumina is a movement of a revivalist nature; it is an art form; it is a part of a total search of at least some of the people for group identity; and it is essentially a return to African religious ideas and concepts of ancestor survival, spirit-possession, sacrifice and racial unity. Any estimate of the real importance of Cumina in Jamaica, a developing society, must take into account the fact that it is not simply a definable theological creed but is concerned with certain incommensurable factors and levels of the human psyche. Cumina is a dimension of spiritual life and aspiration which is in itself elemental and yet transcendental: elemental, in that its roots are in the soil of Africa and in the transplanted spirits of the negroes; transcendental, in that Cumina is not so much a particular belief as an awareness that pervades all the spirits of the participants providing them with some cosmic identity – they are one with the gods, with their ancestral spirits, and with one another. In their drumming, singing, jumping, dancing, rolling and trance they no longer remain separate beings or discrete spirits; they become absorbed into the great Nzambi, the sky-god. Even as an art form Cumina still provides at certain creative levels some sense of identity and purpose.

The Nine-Day Wake

It has been said, and not without some truth, that wakes are pretty much the same the world over, whether held in Africa, Ireland, or the West Indies. Death is a great occasion in Jamaica when sorrow, fear, rejoicing, adulation, confession, story-telling, obscenity, singing, dancing, eating and drinking are all mingled in a long, almost uninterrupted repetition of elemental rituals. Obeah, duppy catching, esoteric rites, formulae – all have their place in the long, seemingly endless wakes which are the inevitable concomitant of a burial in certain areas of Jamaica (such as Ocho Rios), and especially among the rural peasantry. Wakes begin within twenty-four hours after death for hygienic rather than any religious reasons. They are occasions as well as excuses for a general kinship reunion which welcomes at the same time any passing homeless tramp, or interested visitor, who might be looking for entertainment or a free meal.

It is, of course, easy to misconstrue the nine days of the wake as a sort of glorified binge, without order or purpose. In fact, however primitive in form it may be, the Jamaican wake is a carefully ordered and dramatized ritual. Not only does the kin group adjust to the loss of a member, it also ensures that the spirit of the dead person cannot return, unless deliberately recalled by such a ritual as the Cumina. This is achieved, more specifically, by sweeping behind the coffin as it is conveyed to the family or group graveyard, usually situated in the kin-group yard which contains a washroom or washing area, a water tap and a communal latrine as well as a general hut for meetings, games, services and entertainments. The body is finally buried with an eastern orientation, and then the wake really gets under way.

The wake ritual will continue for nine days and most of the nights as well. Everything leads up to the ninth night – referred to as the Nint-Night – when the games, food and African folk stories eventually give way to a ritual of rhythmic music and dancing, the singing of 'sankeys' (that is, hymns from Moody and Sankey), Bible reading and conscienceless flattery of the departed one.

At first sight one element appears to be entirely out of character with the rest of the ritual, namely, the singing of obscene songs, the general mouthing of obscenities and the recounting of bawdy jokes. Fernando Henriques thinks that these activities can be considered as 'an outlet for the fear implicit in any situation concerned with the spirits'. It is certainly not easy to explain obscenity in the context of the wake in teleological terms; and anything so alien to the general tenor of the ritual, especially in comparison with Bible reading and hymn singing, clearly has no theological or philosophical rationale. An explanation of a psychological nature, therefore, seems to be the most likely one. The utterance of obscenities may represent not so much a spirit-directed activity as an expression of bravado in face of the ultimate terror of death itself. It may be a defiant demonstration in the final hours of the Nint-Night that death has at least no power to claim *them,* and their obscenities are an expression of superiority over the dead man who has at last succumbed to the realm of the duppies.

Another explanation at the psychological level may be that the wake is an expression, in microform, of the totality of the life of the participants. In a period of nine days they manage to cover all their normal activities and functions, and the multiplexity of the levels of life. The obscene is no exception. It is a level which, for most of the time, may be kept under control and remains in the regions of the unconscious. The wake is an occasion when the individual, as well as the group, passes through the whole gamut of human emotions which are released in a ritualistic and stylized manner.

The permissibility and acceptance of this particular form of expression make it possible to liberate levels of thought which normally would be resisted and would be regarded as socially unacceptable. Indeed, collective obscenity on these occasions may simply represent a further expression of social and kinship identity at the lowest and most earthy level, just as the hymns, the Bible readings, the prayers, and the Buchmanite-like confessions, or 'sharing', represent a social and spiritual solidarity at a higher, if not the highest, level. Ultimately, the extended family and the kinship group are one at the level of the racial unconscious.

The whole of the 'Nint-Night' ceremony is a period during which the spirit of the dead person seeks to wander back to its home to be entertained by its kinsfolk, and to listen to the final flatteries, before eventually joining the world of the ancestral duppies, or Lomas Land – the land of the Dead. But during this period the very presence of the friends and kinsmen of the departed will ensure his speedy and final return to the grave. In all this the Ninth Night is critical, and those involved in the ceremony have to be particularly vigilant. The exaggerated stories told about the dead person on this last night of the wake are calculated to provide his spirit with as great a send-off as possible; in consequence, a 'nine-night lie' has come to mean a tall story.

It is inevitable, with the progress of the times, the extension of compulsory education, and the increasing sophistication of life generally, that both the nature and the extent of the practice of the wake should be changing. It is universal neither in terms of geography nor in terms of social position. Its practice is far more common in the country areas, in remote villages, than in the towns; and it is observed more frequently by peasants working on the land than by any other groups in society. There is also a tendency for the more intelligent of the younger generation to despise the whole business, as well as any magical or pseudo-magical practices. They regard these occasions as the entertainment and superstitious beliefs of the older generation.

John Canoe Celebrations
Much of what may be said about John Canoe celebrations is of a conjectural nature, and it cannot be fitted naturally into some total

pattern of religious belief. John Canoe is the name given to a form of ceremonial dancing which has been traced back in Jamaica to the late eighteenth century (1774), although the derivation of the term is still very much in doubt. It has been suggested, for example, that the name is derived from the Ewe *dzono,* meaning a magician or sorcerer, and *kunu,* something which is terrible and ugly and may be the cause of death. The traditional pronunciation appears to be Jon Connu, a man who is the central figure in the whole of the celebration. As leader of a troop of dancers he usually wore an elaborate head-dress, representing a house or houseboat, and also a horned mask.

Accounts of the John Canoe celebrations seem to suggest that the dance presented a number of figures or types in a ritualistic way, epitomizing the social hierarchy – if not of Jamaica then possibly of ancient Ashanti – the king and queen, captain (of the army), the clown or court jester, the doctor (sorcerer) and nurse, the warriors and the central, mystical figure of the Bull, or cow-headed man. Indeed, the efficacy of the whole ritual depended upon keeping the identity of this latter secret – he was a tabu figure. It is interesting to note that, although no complete identity with African customs has been established, nor the original meanings of the ceremony elicited, there are many similarities to Ashanti ceremonial dances in which a central figure wore ram's horns, and others (warriors) wore leopard tails.

The John Canoe ceremony was revived in Jamaica in 1851, when a group of dancers, singers and mummers went in procession and made considerable noise with their musical instruments. But there was a general antipathy towards the resuscitation of an apparently pagan ritual whose religious or social significance it was no longer possible (it was felt) even to guess at. Much of the dancing was vulgar in the extreme, and letters appeared in *The Gleaner* insisting upon the suppression of the ceremony. Once again, one can only theorize about the general significance of the proceedings which represented a whole cross-section of human roles and activities. The significance of the houseboat (not canoe) remains a mystery – unless it really has some folklore connexion with a deluge myth and an African Noah hero-figure, as some have suggested. It seems to be a much safer assumption to see in the mystical Bull figure a representation of the African medicine-man, shaman or rain-maker, who is the epitome of the powers of fertility. The houseboat may be suggestive of water; and, in terms of sympathetic magic, the production of a plentiful supply in the rivers through a rain-making ceremony would result in the need for shelter perhaps in a covered boat. This is all, however, largely conjecture, and in so far as the ceremony is still pursued, it is in the spirit of carnival rather than ritual. It is mainly associated with Christmas, and even then it has become less popular over the years; nowadays only a relatively few John Canoe dancers are to be seen in the street.

General Celebrations

Steel drum, steel drum
hit the hot calypso dancing
hot rum hot rum
who goin' stop this bachanalling?
                    Edward Brathwaite, Rights of Passage

The Jamaicans are, like most West Indians, a joyous and spontaneous people who will always convert sorrow and poverty into joy and richness of spirit. We have discussed several ceremonies or festivals – Cumina, the Nine-Day Wake and the John Canoe Celebrations. There are, of course, a number of secular festivals with which we are not particularly concerned here, including the celebration of Independence during the first week of August. In more religious terms, Easter and Christmas are celebrated in much the same way as they are elsewhere; apart from these festivals the only celebrations of any great importance are baptisms and weddings.

During the long years of slavery the planters refused to allow slaves to marry under the aegis of Christian ritual. Whilst the slaves, as we have seen, were given every encouragement to have promiscuous sex relations and to reproduce as fast as possible, they were not encouraged to develop permanent relationships. A planter could always get more money for slaves sold separately than for those put up for auction as man and wife; and, in consequence, 'marriage' of any sort was not encouraged among them. Christian marriage remains an ideal rather than an actuality, and represents the consummation of social ambition and status rather than of love.

In order to fulfil this 'Christian' ideal of marriage it is considered necessary for the prospective bridegroom to have attained a level of social and economic security, which will in turn provide that ethos of respectability which such a marriage demands. In fact, the picture of ideal marriage here envisaged is really a reflection of the planter's home, with its amenities and admirable furnishings and, of course, a servant or two. Not only is the resultant home in such a marriage expensive, but the wedding occasion itself is an opportunity for expansive generosity. It is an occasion for the whole kin group, and in fact the whole village, to participate in the church ritual, when the pair to be married will appear in all their finery and, because they have in all probability been living together for many years, when they will be accompanied by their children.

The wedding festivities, with quite lavish spreads of food and drink, and accompanied by steel bands beating out the happy and improvised calypso songs both to amuse the guests and to embarrass the happy couple, will last as long as the money and refreshments last, and the celebration of one of life's most important contracts will be complete. The sense of celebration itself is not very different from weddings in other societies, although actual invitations are not so strictly organized and the length of the proceedings is not so clearly defined or determined in advance. But the sense of social significance is very different from the more conventional marriages of developed societies, although as time goes on such societies are tending to approximate more closely to the West Indian pattern, with trial periods of cohabitation – of varying length – preceding the marriage ceremony.

Certainly very few of the lowest strata of society are able to get married when they are young because of the formidable expense of such a wedding, and also because of the subsequent standard of living expected. The consummation in a marriage ceremony of almost a lifetime of cohabitation might eventually occur in old age, but it is still considered important, even up to the deathbed, because of its prestige value. It is, in effect, the only form of marriage recognized legally, and it is patriarchal in nature. Christian marriage confers upon the male that legal position and sanction which he appears to lack in society generally. The inability of the 'lower-class' male to support his family in a generous and 'middle-class' manner produces in him a sense of inferiority, and also of subjection to the powerful female elements in the family.

Baptisms are also occasions for great rejoicing and celebration, and it is felt increasingly important to have the blessing of the Church invoked upon the individual, whether infant or adult, and such occasions are an opportunity for the involvement of the whole community in the life of the individual.

Chapter 11
The Rastafarians

The Birth of the Rastafarian Movement
The Rastafarian Movement is one of the most interesting and most difficult of Jamaican religious cults to epitomize. Indeed, it is as much a politico-religious movement as a cult, and whilst its forms are religious its purposes are mainly political. Although it certainly cannot claim a very large following, wherever one goes in Jamaica one can find individual Rastafarians or small cells of followers. It appears to arise mainly among unemployed people who are dissatisfied with their social position and economic conditions. In general terms the movement emphasizes a cultural and spiritual identification with Africa, and it is basically a reaction against domination by the West. Whilst it centres mainly on Kingston it has many adherents outside the Corporate Urban area.

The beginnings of the movement appear to be connected with Marcus Garvey's 'Back to Africa' campaign which began in the early 1930s. Marcus Mosiah Garvey was born in 1887, during a time when the political climate in Jamaica was one of general apathy and lethargy. Jamaican society was in need of a charismatic leader who could organize the people into some sort of united group and inspire corporate hope and both religious and political change. Garvey proved to be such a leader.

He attempted, with a great deal of drive and revivalist oratory, to instil into the black people a pride in their race, colour and country of origin; he was a messiah preaching the possibilities of a new identity based on their archaic beginnings to a people who lacked purpose, unity and self-esteem. In 1918 he established the United Negro Improvement Association with the avowed purpose of improving the lot of the negroes in Africa, the Americas and elsewhere. He hoped also to provide, eventually, complete independence for the black man from white society and the opportunity for him to create his own culture and institutions. His purpose was expressed in the slogan, 'Africa for the Africans at home and abroad; one God, one Aim and one Destiny'. He believed that the only way in which the negro population of Jamaica could really establish its identity was through emigration to Africa and resettlement there.

As a result of Garvey's enthusiastic endeavours a scheme was developed to encourage emigration to Liberia, and gradually the black Jamaicans developed an awareness of their identity, and also the beginnings of a political consciousness. There were some Jamaicans in New York who formed the Jamaican League in order to arouse their brethren to take some positive action. Garvey himself went to America to gain further support for the movement. In 1923, however, as a result of disturbances which ensued from his activities and powerful oratory, he was fined and sentenced to a term of five years imprisonment in the U.S.A., but in 1927 he was deported back to Jamaica. Here he pursued his former activities against all forms of opposition, but soon decided to leave for England where he died in 1940.

Garvey represented for the black man a symbol of hope after a long period of inferiority and helplessness. Even the somewhat distant prospect of 'return' to Africa gave the negro a sense of a future and possible happiness, however remote. The years between 1930 and 1939 were a period of desperation as a result of economic depression and a series of hurricanes which caused considerable devastation. It was during this period that the Rastafarian movement was born and developed, and it is clear that Garvey's programme, which certainly appealed to thousands of negroes in the West Indies, America and Africa, proved an inspiration to the movement.

In 1930 Haile Selassie was crowned Emperor of Ethiopia; and his full title was Ras Tafari, son of Ras Makonem of Harar, King of Ethiopia, Haile Selassie, King of Kings, Lord of Lords, Conquering Lion of the Tribe of Judah. The name Haile Selassie means the Power of the Trinity, and to the Rastafarians he was the 'Living God', 225th in the line of Ethiopian kings in unbroken succession from the Queen of Sheba, who bore King Solomon's son. The title 'Ras' means 'Prince'.

Certainly after Selassie's coronation some Jamaicans began to study their Bibles in greater detail. Prominent among these people were such men as Leonard Howell, Archibald Dunkley, Paul Erlington, Vernal Davis and Ferdinand Ricketts who became the pillars of the Rastafarian movement. Leonard Howell appears to have been the first to introduce the notion that Ras Tafari was the 'Living God'. Howell was a Jamaican by birth and had travelled widely, including in Africa where he was a soldier in the Ashanti war of 1896. He had also travelled in the U.S.A. where he had come into contact with racist tension.

Archibald Dunkley devoted several years to a detailed study of the Bible in an attempt to determine whether Haile Selassie really was the messiah concerning whom Garvey had spoken so much.

Apparently he found confirmation in the Bible, referring to I Timothy vi 13-16:

> I give thee charge in the sight of God, who quickeneth all things, and before Christ Jesus, who before Pontius Pilate witnessed a good confession; that thou keep this commandment without spot, unrebukeable, until the appearing of our Lord Jesus Christ: which in his times he shall show, who is the blessed and only Potentate, the King of Kings, and Lord of Lords; who hath immortality, dwelling in the light which no man can approach unto; who no man hath seen, nor can see: to whom be honour and power everlasting. Amen.

This was further supported by passages in the Book of Revelation, chapters 17 and 19, referring to the Lamb as 'Lord of lords' and 'King of kings', and to the Word of God, who has 'on his vesture and on his thigh a name written, King of kings and Lord of lords'. This belief in Ras Tafari as the messiah inspired them in their early evangelistic work, and militancy came later as a result of the conflict which some of their leaders had with the law.

Thus, the Rastafarians saw in Haile Selassie their Black God, son of the Black Madonna, and Ethiopia became their eschatological hope, their Promised Land. In 1928 Haile Selassie received the title Negus, and this two-syllable word became very popular with the Rastafarians because of the possibility of using it as a substitute for Jesus, as in the following hymns:

> *The Church's one Foundation*
> *Is Negus Christ our Lord;*
> *He is the new creation*
> *By water and the word;*
> *From Heaven he came and sought her*
> *To be his holy bride,*
> *And to one hope she presses*
> *And for her life he lives.*
>
> *Negus shall reign where'er the sun*
> *Does its successive journeys run;*
> *His Kingdom stretch from shore to shore*
> *Till moons shall wax and wane no more.*

It was during the Italian invasion of Ethiopia that the Rastafarians discovered in Revelation xix 16 a further confirmation of the battle of their 'King of kings and Lord of lords' against the powers of evil:

And I saw the beast, and the kings of the earth, and their armies gathered together to make war against him that sat on the horse, and against his army.

When Haile Selassie returned to Ethiopia in 1941 the Rastafarians were convinced that verse 20 had at last literally been fulfilled:

And the beast was taken, and with him the false prophet that wrought miracles before him, with which he deceived them that had received the mark of the beast, and them that worshipped his image. These both were cast alive into a lake of fire burning with brimstone.

The Pinnacle Affair

Under Leonard Howell the movement came into strong conflict with the law of the country. After a variety of somewhat dubious activities (such as selling photographs of Haile Selassie as passports to Ethiopia), Howell was arrested in January 1934, tried and found guilty of uttering seditious language, 'that is, such language as is calculated to cause disturbance and violence among ignorant people'. The Chief Justice stated that he considered Howell was a fraud and sent him to prison for two years.

When Howell was released from prison he organized 'The Ethiopian Salvation Society', which was a branch of a similar society in America, and in 1940 he became the leader of a community at Pinnacle in the parish of St Catherine. About five hundred members of the Society lived at Pinnacle, paying no rent but cultivating the large property there. The main crops of the plantation were yam and ganja or marijuana. In 1941, the police systematically raided Pinnacle, and during these raids some seventy Rastas were arrested for growing ganja or for violence and twenty-eight were sent to prison. Howell was imprisoned again for two years.

In 1953, after a further term of imprisonment, Howell returned to Pinnacle, where he intensified security precautions. From now on many of the Brethren took on the fierce appearance of 'locksmen'; that is, they grew beards and long hair and were referred to as 'Ethiopians' or 'Ethiopian warriors'. They also used ferocious dogs to protect themselves and their property; any stranger who entered their compound was announced by the banging of gongs. In 1954 the Pinnacle was once more raided, 163 members were arrested, and the community was broken up. Howell himself, after making claims to divinity, was committed in 1960 to Kingston Mental Hospital.

The Pinnacle community is regarded as important in the general development of Rastafarianism, since it was here that some of the community rituals and practices began. It was here that the custom of plaiting the hair started, perhaps based on photographs of Somali, Masai, Galla and other tribesmen of Ethiopia. Men who wear their hair in this fashion are usually referred to as 'dreadlocks'.

After the destruction of Pinnacle the residue of the community returned to Kingston to Back-O-Wall or Shanty-Town. There some of them peddled brooms and fruits; some attempted to sell charcoal and firewood; whilst others simply talked to any and every passer-by about their beliefs, their ideas and their social situation. Gradually new groups and communities developed in and around Kingston, and there followed a period of reorganization. Wherever they went their somewhat wild and fanatical appearance attracted an audience; they defied society, shouted profanities and disturbed the peace. Many were arrested.

By the end of 1954 there existed at least twelve Ras Tafari groups in West Kingston alone, ranging from a membership of about twenty to one of about one hundred and fifty. In 1955 Mrs Mami Richardson, one of the leading officials of the Ethiopian World Federation Inc., came to Jamaica to meet local leaders. Her visit resulted in the establishment of many local branches all over Jamaica as well as a statement in September 1955 to the effect that the Emperor Haile Selassie had granted 500 acres of land to the black people of the West who had aided Ethiopia during her struggles against colonialism. It was emphasized that the way in which this land was used would be 'the touchstone for additional grants'. It was also made clear that this was not a signal for the mass migration of the impoverished and disaffected, but an opportunity for those with a pioneering spirit coupled with trade and professional skills.

In 1958 the Rastafarians held a convention, and the press devoted considerable space to its activities. They congregated at their Back-O-Wall headquarters, and there followed nightly rituals of singing and drumming, abuse directed at passing policemen, and many physical clashes with the police. On 24 March, 1958 *The Star* reported:

> The City of Kingston was 'captured' near dawn on Saturday by some 300 bearded men of the Rastafarian cult along with their women and children. About 3.30 a.m., early marketgoers saw members of the Rastafarian movement gathered in the centre of Victoria Park, with towering poles atop of which fluttered black, green and red banners, and

loudly proclaiming that they had captured the city.... When the police moved toward them, a leader of the group with hands raised issued a warning to the police: 'Touch not the Lord's anointed'.... The police finally removed them.

During the ensuing months after the Convention there was a general increase of tension between the government and the Rastafarians. Many were arrested under the Jamaican Dangerous Drug Law for using ganja, and there were many searches and much harassment. In 1959 the camp of Prince Edward on Spanish Town Road, which was the former Back-O-Wall area, was raided; all the Rastas there were arrested and the camp was burnt down. After their trial the men were set free. But by then both social scientists and the more socially aware politicians realized that they were dealing here with a problem which went beyond the fanaticism of a small group of people. Their aspirations, however expressed, could no longer be ignored.

The Claudius Henry Affair

It is inevitable that such a movement as that of the Rastafarians should throw up a variety of leaders, many of them in opposition to one another, forming splinter groups with different and developing ideals. There was, for example, one leader named Claudius Henry, a Jamaican who had been living in America and who was, in fact, ordained there, and became involved in the Ethiopian World Federation Inc. He resigned, however, from this Federation and in 1959 returned to Jamaica where he became the founder of a new African movement called the African Reform Church whose headquarters were in West Kingston.

In March 1959, Henry – the 'Repairer of the Breach' – distributed a large number of cards or tickets to members of the public in Jamaica. Some of these cards are still extant, and they read as follows:

> FREE 'GOD'S RIGHTEOUS KINGDOM' CERTIFICATE OF MEMBERSHIP 'THE LEPERS GOVERNMENT'
>
> From the Ancient and Mythical Realm of Neptune Rex, Court of the Dawn, 'The Rod and Star', 'Ensign', 'The Red, Gold and Green' with the morning star in the centre.
>
> Know all ye by these present that I............
>
> And my family of............................
>
> Address................
>
> are registered members of the African Reform Church of God in

Christ, The first fruit House of Prayer. Founder and Pastor, Rev. C.V. Henry, R.B. with 'The Seventh Emanuel's Brethren'. Administrating 'The Lepers Government' under the United Ethiopian Pilgrim's Pioneer Movement. Pioneering Israel's scattered Children of African Origin back home to Africa, this year 1959, deadline date Oct. 5th. This New Government is God's Righteous Kingdom of Everlasting Peace on Earth. 'Creation's Second Birth'. Holder of this Certificate is requested to visit the Headquarters at 78 Rosalie Ave., off Waltham Park Road, August 1st 1959, for our Emancipation Jubilee, commencing 9a.m. sharp.

Please preserve this Certificate for removal. No passport will be necessary for those returning home to Africa.

Bring this Certificate with you on August 1st for 'Identification'.

'The Seventh Emmanuel's Brethren' gathering Israel's Scattered Children for removal.

Leader, God's Appointed and Anointed Prophet, Rev. C.V. Henry, R.B.

Given this 2nd day of March 1959, in the year of the reign of His Imperial Majesty, 1st Emperor of Ethiopia. 'God's Elect', Haile Selassie, King of Kings and Lord of Lords. Israel's Returned Messiah.

There were thousands who believed not only that Haile Selassie was their Returned Messiah but also that Claudius Henry was about to lead them into the Promised Land. By 5 October, 1959, hundreds of Jamaicans had flocked from all over the country to 78 Rosalie Avenue, Kingston, in readiness to depart at once for Africa. But the promised emigration to Ethiopia did not take place; the deadline date came and passed, and Claudius Henry could do nothing. He argued, somewhat unconvincingly, that 5 October was never intended to be the day for the great Exodus from bondage, but rather the day on which the government of Jamaica would explain how it would meet the demands of the 'Seventh Emmanuel's Brethren'. Henry was arrested, but he was eventually set free by the Court which seemed to regard him more as a religious fanatic than as a political agitator. He was bound over to keep the peace for a year and fined £100.

Henry, however, had not learned his lesson, and he became increasingly hostile towards the government and the status quo generally. On 7 April, 1960, he was arrested with nine of his followers, and a large number of weapons and a variety of ammunition were seized at his headquarters. This affair is referred to as 'the infamous Henry rebellion' or 'the Henry fiasco', and the leader himself as 'the seditious Henry', although he would still strongly deny any political or seditious intention. Henry was convicted and sentenced to a long term of imprisonment; but his followers, who were regarded more as simple dupes of the great Henry, received sentences which were much lighter. The struggle, however, was not over and Henry's son Ronald took up the fight which ended in disaster when two soldiers of the Royal Hampshire Regiment were killed after violent clashes with Henry supporters. Ronald and four of his followers were sentenced to death.

As a result of the Henry affairs, and of the general disturbances and unrest that ensued, the Government decided to have a full investigation into the problems faced by the various Rastafarian communities. This investigation was a short but very intensive one carried out by a mixed group of professional sociologists and nominated Rastafarians. They made their report to the Government in 1960, and it was unanimous in its recommendations, even if there was some divergence of opinion about the actual situation. The recommendations included the following:

> 1. A mission should be sent to certain countries in Africa in order to investigate the possibilities of Jamaican emigration to some, if not all, of these countries. There should be a fair representation of members of the various Rastafarian movements in this mission.
>
> 2. Discussions with Rastafarians concerning the preparations for such a mission should be initiated immediately.
>
> 3. It should be made clear to the general public that the investigations which had been carried out revealed that the majority of Rastafarians were peaceful citizens who were quite willing to work.
>
> 4. Any security enquiries that still remained for the police to make should be made quickly, and they should cease to persecute those Rastafarians who were clearly pursuing their lives peacefully together.
>
> 5. There should be an acceleration in the construction of low-rent houses, and much more encouragement to people generally to develop self-help, co-operative building schemes.
>
> 6. There should be some attempt to provide and develop water, lighting and sewerage systems in the areas in which the Rastafarians had

squatted and established living quarters.

7. An increasing number of civic centres should be developed with facilities for youth clubs, child clinics and classes in technical subjects. In this all-out effort it was suggested that the churches and the (then) University College of the West Indies should collaborate.

8. The Ethiopian Orthodox Coptic Church should be invited to establish a branch in West Kingston.

9. The Rastafarians should be given every aid to establish co-operative workshops.

10. Both press and radio facilities should be accorded to leading members of the Rastafarian movement.

As a direct consequence of these recommendations the Jamaican Government sent a mission to Africa on 4 April, 1961. It spent one week in Ethiopia, two weeks in Nigeria, one week in Ghana, six days in Liberia, and finally one week in Sierra Leone, returning to Jamaica on 2 June, 1961. A further delegation was sent to Africa in 1962. These visits established the fact that those African countries which were prepared to receive Jamaicans had three chief areas of need: immigrants who had professional or technical qualifications; artisans with specific skills; Jamaicans with real and skilled farming experience. The visit of 1962 was more specifically concerned with questions of trade and cultural exchange.

The sad and tragic 'Henry affair' had ultimately led to some positive proposals with regard to emigration to Africa, although these were strictly limited and certainly not very helpful or encouraging to the mass of Rastafarians.

The Various Rastafarian Movements
The Rastafarian movement is one which derives from a mass desire to break off the shackles of white domination, which was to be replaced by the similar supremacy of a black elite seeking to imitate very closely European culture. It is, however, one thing to know in general terms what one is against, but it is quite another to be able to state, in precise terms, what one is for. There is, as it has perhaps already become clear, no one single Rastafarian movement, but a heterogeneous collection of movements. There is certainly no consensus amongst Rastafarians as to precisely what it is they believe, or even what it is they all want from their Jamaican society. There are those who claim that their movement is essentially non-political and non-subversive. They still

remember some of the very real tragedies that resulted for many people from the Henry affair. Whilst they may have no wish to co-operate or compromise with the government, they also have no desire to attack or oppose the government in any way that might be construed as seditious. The author spoke to one Rastafarian in the Cockpit country who was quite convinced that he was being pursued and cross-questioned by M.I.5.

Yet another group wish to co-operate with the government in a limited way. This is by no means motivated by a desire to help the government or to aid in any way the improvement of Jamaican society, but rather by a belief that this cooperation would hasten the government's decision to 'repatriate' the whole of the Jamaican-African-Israelites. Others undoubtedly would still, in the Ronald Henry tradition, like to gain political power in Jamaica – though not necessarily by force.

There are still others who seek their full human rights within the Jamaican society; not, however, in order to take on responsibilities or to participate more fully in the total social political situation, but simply as a preparation for the ultimate repatriation of all who hope to go to Africa. Their prayer is that their enemies will at last release them to return to their Promised Land, or even that their 'captors' might all pass away:

> Deliver us from the hands of our enemies, that we might prove fruitful for the last days. When our enemies are passed and decayed in the depths of the sea, in the depths of the earth or in the belly of a beast, oh, give us all a place in Thy Kingdom for ever and ever. Selah!

The chief Rastafarian groups have been identified as follows:

The Human Rights Brethren Association of Barbican, St Andrew

This group has a small membership, is weak in its organisation and is still struggling to develop. It has not really at any time fully clarified either its short-term or its long-term objectives. Its members feel, on the whole, that they are denied freedom of speech and of assembly, that the new Jamaica is little more than a modernized form of colonialism in its aspirations. They complain bitterly about the levels of opportunity and education offered to the black man in developing Jamaica, and feel that the government is making inadequate provision for certain classes in their society.

The Rastafarian Movement, African Recruitment Centre, Kingston

This group lived formerly in the Dungle or Dung Hill, a crowded, unhealthy area in West Kingston, filled with shacks mainly of wood and corrugated iron. Their leader was originally one Samuel Brown who was their candidate for West Kingston in the election campaign of 1961. Brown claimed that the only way for the black man to achieve his aim in Jamaica was to seize power through politics; but he gained only eighty-five votes in the election. In April 1966 gang warfare broke out and Brown was arrested and imprisoned. In July of the same year the government undertook 'Operation Shanty Town' during which the unhygienic shacks of the Rastafarian group were destroyed.

The central ideas of this movement are summed up in the captions 'One God, One Aim, One Destiny', 'All black men are brothers' and 'The Rastafarian is he who will never relinquish the fact that he is African'. Their persistent prayer, recited at all their meetings, is as follows:

> Princes shall come out of Egypt, Ethiopia shall stretch forth her hand unto God. Oh thou God of Ethiopia, thou God of thy divine majesty, thy spirit come within our hearts to dwell in the path of righteousness. That the hungry be fed, the sick nourished, the aged protected, the infant cared for. Help us to forgive that we may be forgiven. Teach us love and loyalty as it is in Zion. Deliver us from the hand of our enemy that we may prove fruitful for the last day, when our enemy has passed, and decayed in the depth of the sea or in the belly of a beast. O give us a place in thy Kingdom for ever and ever. So we hail our God, Selassie I, Jehovah God, Ras Tafari, Almighty God, Ras Tafari, Great and Terrible God, Ras Tafari, who sitteth in Zion and reigneth in the hearts of men and women, hear and bless us and sanctify us, and cause thy loving face to shine upon us thy children that we may be saved. Selah.

Samuel Brown was responsible for the development of the twenty-one points forming a document called the *Foundation of the Rastafarian Movement*. The main tenor of these points may be summed up as follows:

> (a) The Rastafarian Movement is opposed to any form of discrimination against, or oppression of, the black population of Jamaica.

> (b) It stands for the fullest freedom and the recovery of the dignity, self-respect and sovereignty of the black people.

> (c) The black man must have the same opportunity for housing, food,

education and employment as the white or brown man.

(d) The Rastafarian Movement has as its chief aim the complete destruction of all vestiges of white supremacy in Jamaica, thereby ending economic exploitation and the social degradation of the black people.

(e) The Movement stands for repatriation and power, and for the fullest co-operation and intercourse between both governments and peoples of Africa and a free and independent people of Jamaica.

(f) The Movement has decided actively to join the political struggle and to create a political movement with the aim of *taking power*.

(g) Opposition to the political leadership of white men and brown men is not because of their colour but because of the wickedness they represent. All men, irrespective of colour, are free to join this political crusade provided that they abandon evil.

The Rastafarian Repatriation Association of Jamaica

This particular group was originally led by Brother Mack, who had been one of the original members of the Mission to Africa in 1961. The group regards Africa, and the black man generally, as the future saviour of the world, responsible, as indicated in Revelation vi 6, for the bringing of justice and healing to mankind: 'And when he had opened the third seal, I heard the third beast say, Come and see. I beheld and lo a black horse; and he that sat on him had a pair of balances in his hand'. Brother Mack saw the world becoming embroiled in a nuclear war in which the European nations would destroy themselves, after which the black people of the world would all return to Africa and live in peace. Europe and America represent the Babylon, the mother of harlotry and intrigue, in the book of Revelation. The great cry of this movement is 'Uhuru', which is Swahili for 'Freedom'. Count Ossie's Rastafarian Bongo Band is one of the more colourful features of the Association, which is also noted for its ritualistic war-dances. Its Declaration of Policy contains seven points:

(a) To promote the repatriation to Africa of all members.

(b) To promote the spiritual and religious knowledge of the Solomonic dynasty founded by King Solomon and the Queen of Sheba.

(c) To promote educational progress of the African continent, its languages, culture and history.

(d) To recognize the hurt suffered by the Continent of Africa through colonialism and to devote time and energy towards the development of Africa by all possible contributions.

(e) To promote the general welfare of members.

(f) To assist members to recuperate from ill-health and provide medical attention wherever necessary.

(g) To collect voluntary subscriptions and contributions to carry out its purpose.

The Ethiopian African Congress and Rastafarian Melchezedec Orthodox Church

The particular message of this group is 'Peace and Love', and it has links – however tenuous – with the Ethiopian Orthodox Coptic Church. Their services are marked by considerable dramatization and ritual. The group is completely dissatisfied with its treatment by both the Jamaican government and the police who raid it repeatedly. In 1963 their camp was burned to the ground and was destroyed completely in 1966.

The Ras Tafari Brethren United Front

This group claims that it has no political affiliations or ideologies; it refuses to make any compromises with society or with the government; it is non-subversive, non-violent and non-abusive; and it is essentially a cultural movement seeking identity in and through a common destiny in the Promised Land of Ethiopia.

When Haile Selassie came to Jamaica on 21 April, 1966, it was claimed by one eye-witness that no fewer than 100,000 people came to the airport to meet him, and that of these at least 10,000 were Rastafarians. At last their King Messiah had come to them in Babylon itself, out of the Promised Land, their Ethiopic Zion, to which they all hoped one day to return. The visit of His Imperial Majesty, Ras Tafari, the King of Kings and Lord of Lords, lent a certain prestige to the cause of the black tribes of Israel living in captivity.

Practices and Beliefs of Rastafarians

It is not easy to summarize the beliefs of such a heterogeneous group of people as the Rastafarians. There are, however, a number of common beliefs which are held by most of the Rastafarians whatever their sectarian allegiances. Haile Selassie is for all of them the Living Black God, despite his death; black is beautiful, good and holy – 'So we hail our God, Selassie I, Eternal God, Ras Tafari: hear us and help us, and cause thy face to shine upon us thy children'. Ethiopia is heaven, the Promised Land, whilst Jamaica and any other country outside of Ethiopia are a part of Babylon, a living hell. In this living hell the Rastafarians represent the lowest element in Jamaican society, and some of the Brethren avoid society and its complexities as much as possible; they have become separatists. Others accept the total situation since they feel that there is nothing that they can do about it. Still others become aggressive towards society and seek in some positive way to disrupt it and bring about its final destruction.

Since black is holy and beautiful, white must be evil, ugly and inferior; and to the Rastafarian the white man is so inferior that there is no longer any possibility of working for him. This belief, in effect, prevents the Rastafarian from doing any sort of work unless he can be employed by other Rastafarians. The black man is the reincarnation of the Ancient Israelites, and he has been in exile in Jamaica for many years through the cruelty and captivity of the white man. In this respect the white man has been used by God to punish the Israelites through slavery. Many Rastafarians will certainly accept that there have been through the ages a number of appearances by God in the form of such saviours as Moses, Elijah and Jesus Christ. The advent of Haile Selassie I is regarded as the climax of God's revelation to man, and we are now in the age of theocracy – the rule of God on earth. This rule will be centred in Ethiopia where they believe preparations are being made for expatriated Africans to return to Ethiopia, their Zion; and in the near future the black man will govern the world, and the white man will become the black man's servant.

The Rastafarian groups have their own organization and hierarchical structure. At the head of any group is a leading brother or priest who is responsible for convening meetings. He is assisted by a chaplain who opens meetings with a religious service and closes them with songs, chants and benedictions. The recording secretary, who very occasionally may be a woman, takes the minutes of the meeting, presides over roll calls and makes a note of members' subscriptions. The treasurer is in charge of all the funds of the group; and the sergeant-at-arms is there to guard the gate at all the meetings in order to prevent the intrusion of police or unauthorized snoopers, particularly when ganja is being smoked.

Ganja is referred to as the 'herb' or 'wisdom weed', which they believe was found growing on the grave of King Solomon. Today it is cultivated throughout Jamaica, and every so often the police conduct a full-scale raid on a particular area. Cigarettes containing ganja are referred to as 'spliffs', and they are smoked widely by people other than Rastafarians in some of the 'yard' dancing activities. The Jamaicans will argue that smoking ganja is less dangerous than drinking white rum or even smoking tobacco.

A considerable proportion of Rastafarians have been brought up in a 'Christian' home, which means that they have been taught to read or recite passages from the Bible, particularly the Old Testament. To them the Bible is a book of symbols to which the Rastafarians alone have the key. All the Old Testament prophecies and the eschatological visions of the book of Revelation are interpreted in terms of Rastafarian beliefs and expectations. This all leads to a somewhat ambivalent view of Christianity, in which the Hebrew Messianic expectations are shared, but the Christ is no longer identified with the Jesus of the New Testament; he is now the Negus of Ethiopia. The Rastafarians in general oppose the Christian faith as practised in Jamaica. For them the churches are merely a Sunday affair 'where the white preachers appeared for an hour and disappeared until the next Sunday'. The white ministers, and some of the white educators, remain as the last remnant and ever-present reminder of British imperialism in Jamaica.

'Christianity' still means for the Rastafarian the old world of slavery; and even the white man's Bible has been simply a tampering with, through translation of, the original Amharic, the language of Ethiopia. In particular, the Roman Catholic Church is the Beast, the Harlot of Babylon, which must eventually be destroyed. And just as the Italian invasion of Ethiopia was predicted (Rev xix 19), and the return of the Emperor to Ethiopia in 1941 (Rev xix 20-1), so the rest of the history of the black man is to be found fully and precisely predicted in the New Testament – all that it requires is some interpretation in Rastafarian terms.

Rastafarians feel that it is their duty to spread the beliefs and hopes which they hold to all black Jamaicans. They do this by holding meetings in the street in a most casual sort of way. A couple will start a discussion and gradually the crowds will gather round to hear the good-humoured wit, the prophetic fire and the intense conviction of the orators. In one town which the author visited the Town Crier was himself a Rastafarian, and he made use of his authority and his powers of rhetoric to draw the crowds and then to expound the mysteries of the Scriptures which the white man had so vilely and violently misinterpreted. God was black; the Christian Church was Babylon, the Beast, the

Devil Incarnate; the Jamaican negroes were the Elect who would eventually be transported by their God Messiah to the Promised Land.

Their meetings are frequently referred to as *grounation,* a conflation of the words 'ground' and 'foundation'. The idea is that the group receives a grounding in the Spirit of God through which they develop agreement or consensus on their ideas, beliefs and plans. In this spirit of identity they participate in communal ganja smoking by passing a ganja-filled pipe around the circle of disciples. This resembles in some ways the smoking of the 'pipe of peace' of North American Indians, and corresponds also to the Holy Communion of the Christian Church. The love and peace of the Brethren is experienced in these ritualistic activities, including the sharing of simple food such as flour and macaroni mixed with water. There follows a period of 'jollification' or happiness.

As already indicated there is considerable variety among the Rastafarians, not only in their beliefs and hopes but also in their appearance and social participation. There are those among the men who are referred to as 'dreadlocks' or 'locksmen'; they grow their beards and their hair long, as they imagine Ethiopian warriors still do who are members of such tribes as the Somali, Masai and Galla. Their long plaited hair is regarded as a symbol of authority, approved by God, the flowing robe and accompanying staff are quite typical of the locksmen. But there are other young Rastafarians who are referred to as 'clean-faced' or 'clippies', many of whom come from better-class homes and have had secondary and even university education. Through their general sense of frustration they find themselves attracted to Rastafarianism, although they have certain limits beyond which they will not go – at least for the present – in relation to their personal appearance.

Rastafarianism is a predominatingly male cult, and women are not only held in a subordinate position, but also regarded as inferior to the male. To some extent the movement is not only political and religious but also psychological; it represents a male protest against the matriarchal structure of a great deal of Jamaican family life, which is founded and rooted in slavery itself. It is strongly felt that the 'Christian' form of marriage is not really part of the black man's world – it belongs to the white man's society and culture, not to his. To the Rastafarian, woman is basically evil, and man's failure is essentially her fault. She is changed and cleansed by association with her mate – which is not a loving relationship, but merely a sexual one. Indeed, association with the woman may be redeeming for her, but it is also a degradation of her very womanhood. There is no formal marriage in terms of a religious or civil ceremony, but simply what is known as a 'changing of hands', whereby a woman is taken to wife in the name of His Imperial Majesty Haile Selassie. Birth control is tabu for Rastafarians, since for them this is a device of the white man to destroy the black population; it is also a means to prevent the reincarnation of the Lost Tribes of Israel upon earth. They do, indeed, look after their children with some care, and seek to bring them up as Rastafarians.

The Essential Nature of Rastafarianism

It is suggested by some that the cult is not really a messianic one, but certainly the concept of a messiah is there, and Haile Selassie has fulfilled for all Rastafarians this particular function. Their common hope is still that the Negus will be their messiah not only in terms of the 'Anointed One' of God, but also in terms of a saviour and redeemer who will eventually lead them to the Promised Land. A messianic cult implies a unity in revolt against society as it is, and in favour of an alternative that has been predicted and previsioned – just as the early Christian faith was essentially a messianic cult. Every Rastafarian treasures a photo of Haile Selassie who is both his Christ and his God. Through the redemption which the Negus brings they will experience the end of their 'Babylonian Captivity' and the enslaving power of the white Beast. Final freedom will be found upon returning to the sacred soil of Zion, the Land of Ethiopia:

> *Africa awaken, morning is at hand,*
> *No more art thou forsaken, Ethiopia now is free.*

Rastafarianism is more of an escapist movement than a revolutionary one. Society with all its complexities and problems had become insupportable for the poverty-stricken peasants of Jamaica, and they had either to withdraw within themselves or become the originators of an escapist group with common hatreds and identifiable hopes. They began, therefore to escape from their present world into an unreal world of their own mental construction.

Escapism can be at a variety of levels – the psychological, the sociological or the religious. As an escapist movement Rastafarianism finds its followers at all these levels: those who desire desperately to escape from themselves, their failures and their inadequacies; those who have found society intolerable, unfulfilling and quite incapable of satisfying their social and economic needs amid chronic unemployment; and those whose Christian training and background has failed them, who find their lives empty and without purpose and so seek out some distant messiah, beyond their reach and perhaps even beyond their wildest hopes, to escape to an unrealizable Paradise.

Some have suggested that Rastafarianism is a 'nativistic' movement. This means that it is an attempt by a virtually cultureless people (or a people who are culturally deprived) to construct a culture of their own, partly by harking back to those native elements in their own harassed, disturbed, truncated and emasculated history; and partly by a deliberate attempt to revitalize their present situation by the production of a new, if artificial, culture. This is done initially by the rejection of contemporary society, and by increased aggravation of the social and political situation. In the distorted cultural ambiance that results, the attempt is made to reject and eliminate all alien influences, customs and individuals from their way of life.

The initial result of all this is an incredible confusion, since the attempt to recreate an 'African culture' frequently implies something that no longer exists in any pure form in Africa itself, but is merely an artificially preserved archaism. The whole question of African culture requires much closer scrutiny, discrimination and description than most Rastafarians are prepared to give it. African identity remains a vague, somewhat featureless and ill-defined concept which has become a sort of apotheosis of an aboriginal dream-time with details to suit each wandering Rastafarian imagination. As a nativistic movement it is a *conscious,* almost self-conscious, one organized by its members to invoke only certain elements in their cultural past for resurrection and artificial promotion.

Deprivation, with the despair that accompanies and follows it, has helped to make the movement at least a pseudo-political one. There is a cause of a political nature, however inadequate or irrelevant the Rastafarian movement may be for its support and final resolution. It is, in consequence, dysfunctional in that although it opposes social ills and deprivation it does not seek to rectify those ills, since this would destroy its very raison d'etre. It acts, therefore, as an irritant, socially and politically looking for its own millennium, not in active social reconstruction but in a dream paradise materialized by an Ethiopian messiah.

The International Peacemakers 'Association

What has just been said may be true of the *total* movement, but it is not absolutely true of all branches or groups within Rastafarianism. Odd though it may seem, the most positive social contribution made by any Rastafarian sect in recent years has been by Claudius Henry himself. After his release from prison he founded the *International Peacemakers' Association* which has several branches in Jamaica. Its aim is primarily religious; as Henry puts it, 'to establish peace in the earth'. He has completely given up his 'Back to Africa Movement', but maintains that he still receives opposition from the government.

His association remains a limb of the larger Rastafarian movement, but it does not share the present aim to use violence to achieve its goals. It seeks mutual understanding between blacks and whites, although according to Henry the whites are not yet ready for his message. The Christian Church, he suggests, is not leading us into the Kingdom: if the Church Confession is right, and 'we have left undone the things we ought to have done and there is no health in us', then it is time we began to do the right things and become healthy. God is goodness, and that goodness is both in man and expressed through man. In 1960 the Jamaican government took away from Henry his ordination certificate, his preacher's licence and his passport. He is barred, he avers, from all forms of public speaking outside the limits of his own private property; he is not allowed to write for the press, speak on the radio, in the street or in a church, or appear in television interviews. In consequence, Henry has taken on increasingly the role of resident prophet, guru and leader in his own Association.

In 1936, when he was thirty-three, Henry was arrested on the information, he claims, of a white minister, for preaching against the churches. He was charged with 'lunacy' and locked up in prison. There the Spirit of God came to him and told him that he would remain there for three days and then return home. During that time he was to eat and drink nothing that was offered to him. He was examined by three doctors and the critical issue appeared to be the question as to whether the visions he claimed to have were a symptom of some mental disorder or whether they represented some inexplicable religious reality. His main vision appeared to be the repetition of Christ's crucifixion in the East, suggesting that Christ was being, or was about to be, crucified afresh. The third doctor who examined him was apparently very sympathetic towards him, and felt that Henry possessed the key to the whole future situation.

Whilst Henry still feels that he was subsequently 'framed' he accepts resignedly that the 'Back to Africa' concept was a misinterpretation of the prophetic visions he had. Haile Selassie is still accorded respect as 'King of Kings and Lord of Lords', Israel's Returned Messiah and direct descendant of King Solomon and the Queen of Sheba, and Ethiopia remains for him the New Jerusalem or Zion, but it is no longer a part of his plan or that of the Association's to return to Ethiopia. Yet Henry has never really learned the lesson that a prophet is safe only so long as he is not too precise in his prophecies, particularly in relation to dates; and, moreover, that such prophecies should be amenable to a variety of interpretations.

The farcical deadlines which he gave in 1959 should have taught him that eschatology is a dangerous business and that it has led many a would-be messiah or leader to an inglorious and ignominious end. But, whilst his heart is 'full of peace and love', Henry knows that in the end his sufferings and sacrifice, the execution of his son and the brutal murder of his wife, will be avenged; that he 'must win' and that God's wrath is hastening on. He predicted that after 1 April, 1972, peace would come from Jamaica to the rest of the world, and that God 'would make wars to cease unto the ends of the earth'. If this particular prophet never learns, he has at least one enduring and endearing quality – he never gives up and is never discouraged. He is a man who has had a vision and knows that he is 'the key' to his people's future.

April 1972, however, has long since come and gone; there are still many wars and rumours of war, and peace has certainly not come to the world in general or to Jamaica in particular. But whilst Claudius Henry may continually lack something on the prophetic side, on the practical side he still seeks to fulfil his vision of Jamaica's future, despite dissension in his own ranks.

Within the community which he is building up Henry has developed a large bakery from which a fleet of vans is sent around selling bread and cakes to shops. This is the main centre of activity, and the profits which accrue from this enterprise are ploughed back into the other work of the Association. This includes the building of simple and cheap, but well-constructed, homes for community members, an all-age school, an industrial school to teach trades to children beyond school-leaving age, and a secondary school. The object of the whole project is to make people self-supporting and to develop within them some self-respect. Certainly the conditions of work are good in this particular Rastafarian society; a canteen is provided, and the children in the community seemed, in 1971, both well-behaved and in sound health. Indeed, many children were and still are, coming in from outside the community to learn, to play and to eat.

In all the activity of building, which includes a Headquarters and Hall for the Association, the 'Repairer of the Breach' really feels that at last he is beginning to understand 'the key' to the whole of his mission; he is repairing the waste places, making them fertile and bringing in the Kingdom. When all his buildings are ready the world will have to come to Claudius Henry because he is the holder of 'the key', which leads to the ultimate truth of all things. He has, within the precincts of the Association's Headquarters, his wife's tomb, the Ten Commandments, Aaron's Rod, the Ark of the Covenant, twelve stones representing the Twelve Tribes of Israel, the Bright and Morning Star of King David, and Ebenezer – the Stone of Help. Ethiopia may be Zion, but it is a Zion which is no longer within reach; 'the key' makes Jamaica itself the new Zion; it is the final realization of the visions which came to Henry during nine days of fasting before he was imprisoned in 1936, when the Archangel Gabriel appeared to him with the secrets of the future. It is the key to the future of Jamaica, of the black man, and of the whole of mankind.

The lesson of Claudius Henry is an interesting one, and it is the story of a project that is by no means finished. It is essentially the story of a man of burning conviction, with a sense of mission, and with a history of persecution, rejection and suffering. And yet it is the story of a man who, with all his failures, the accusations of sedition, and the pathetic inability to fulfil promises and prophecies, still had a commitment to a much misused and maltreated people, and a willingness to become involved, socially as well as spiritually, in their day-to-day problems.

The Rastafarians and Jamaican Society

Whatever else the Rastafarians are or are not, they have a certain vitality all their own. It is true that, as a movement, they are totally antagonistic to Christianity in general as expressed by white people in the West, and to Catholicism in particular. Whilst they speak without fear and without compromise it also remains true that when one examines some of their tenets, their quite unhistorical statements about their own past culture, as well as their cavalier, ignorant and uncritical approach to the Bible, one gets the impression of a group of people who are quite prepared to manipulate facts to suit their own purpose.

They are vehement in their attacks on the government, the white man, imperialism and Christianity, and their eloquence is touched by that naivete which derives, for the most part, from an almost total ignorance of the world, economic affairs, and any sense of history. This is not to say that they do not have a cause; it is simply to state that whatever case they may have, they parody it with their odd speech, dress and behaviour. Some of them certainly possess a strange dignity of carriage which belongs to a different world; others are comical figures, out of place and out *of* joint both in Jamaica and in their longed-for Zion, Ethiopia. Many of them are amusing, with a trenchant sense of humour; some are grimly fanatical, their fanaticism being fed by smoking the ganja weed, which gives them a strange, other-worldly, even prophetic look at times. And if their interpretation and exposition of Biblical texts are novel, they still manage to capture and enchant their audiences, despite their show of contempt for both black and white authority.

There can be no question about the socio-religious importance of the movement in Jamaican society. Its estimated following in 1970 was between 70,000 and 100,000, of whom 80 per cent were between seventeen and thirty-five years of age. Nine years later they show little sign of any reduction in numbers. They are to be found, in cells, throughout the whole of Jamaican society, and although membership has been in the past essentially lower class, a more recent trend in the movement includes frustrated young people from secondary schools and the university who see no future in the island and are becoming the intellectuals of the Rastas.

As long as its millenarian hopes lie in Africa, however, the movement in general must remain sterile and with little real power to change Jamaican society. Jamaica remains, to all intents and purposes, a part of the white man's Babylon, and so (in their view) not worth redeeming. By virtue of its own doctrines it could do little to change society or the direction of the development of Jamaican culture. So long as social deprivation exists they have an effective complaint and something to oppose; but should society change and improve, their mode of living and living conditions would also improve, or at least could improve – and they would lose their social raison d'etre.

And when one looks at the total Rastafarian situation there still remains that one persistent, prophetic, perhaps even self-deluded figure of Claudius Henry who seeks by every means to better the social and environmental situation of his people. No longer in the mainstream of Rastas, the failed apocalyptic figure, chastened by almost insupportable suffering, shows his concern for his people by organizing, planning and working as well as teaching, preaching and divining the future. The man who shouted 'Back to Africa' is at last demonstrating that true life and living is here and now with God in each man, showing what is best in human relationships by living and working for the other.

The Death of Haile Selassie and the Presence of Black Power

Haile Selassie's death in 1975 might, perhaps, be seen as the end of Rastafarian hopes and beliefs. But human beings with religious hopes and expectations are very resilient, as Claudius Henry has demonstrated. The tomb was not the end of Christ for his followers; nor, indeed, was his ascension after resurrection – he would come again to rule in majesty and have dominion over the earth. During the first century after Christ there was current a myth about Nero Caesar – he was not dead, but was hiding somewhere in the East, whence he would most certainly return riding at the head of Parthian hordes, conquering and eventually taking dominion over the whole world. *Nero redivivus* was a hope nourished in almost the same way as in the present century many fanatical Nazis have been quite unable to accept the death of Adolf Hitler but have believed that he would one day surprise the world with his return. The myth of the death and return of the hero-god is perennial in human cultures, and it requires no further detailed exemplification here.

There are ambivalent attitudes towards the 'reported death' of Haile Selassie among the Rastafarians. There are those who believe that he is still alive, and who regard the whole thing as a trick or a plot designed to destroy their hopes of ever being released from 'Babylon', and to reduce in consequence their political and anti-social activities to a minimum. But whilst they do recognize that certain changes have taken place in Ethiopia, they believe that their beloved Ras Tafari is still in full command.

There are those, however, who are quite logical in their approach to the theological problem. Man can destroy the physical body of the 'Divine', but not the divine spirit itself. Negus will return in power to redeem his faithful followers from the slavery of 'Babylon', and he will rule over the conquered earth in majesty. Indeed, nothing has really changed except that their god is no longer physically present: he is omnipresent in spirit and will come in the clouds with the hosts of heaven. Just as the death of Christ is seen by the Church as part of the theology of Incarnation, so the death of Haile Selassie has been absorbed, or is in the process of being absorbed, into the Rastafarian eschatology. *Negus redivivus* is really no more of a problem than *Christus redivivus*; their eternal and spiritual hope remains. As one Rasta disk-recording boldly affirms, 'Jah Live'. In the same way, too, the concept of Ethiopia is spiritualized.

The emphasis on the concept of *negritude,* and on 'black is beautiful', among the Rastafarians might at first blush suggest some involvement in the Black Power movement. Little evidence has, however, been adduced to suggest that this is so, and those elements of Black Power that exist are mainly non-religious in origin, but derive from a rather small Marxist and anti-white group. Their activities are not specifically relevant to this book; but it is true to say that among somewhat disaffected groups, such as the Rastafarians, there is always the potential material for revolution, once it has been turned away from its in-built negativism towards positive social attitudes. In general, there is evidence that some educated youngsters from the middle classes support Black Power from socio-economic and political conviction, whilst there is an increasing number of alienated and generally disaffected middle-class youth who tend to give some support, however superficial, to the Rastafarian movement. Black Power is thus not developing strongly in Jamaica, and black nationalist sentiment has largely given way to socialist ideology, which, while not ignoring racial discrimination, does not highlight it.

Chapter 12
Christian Sects and Denominations

During some research which the author did in Jamaica in the summer of 1971, something like 127 different denominations, sects and individual churches with their own specific names and titles were noted (see Appendix One). It must be made clear, however, that many of these so-called 'sects' represent simply the outcome of internal divisions among some of the larger groups; and some churches are quite clearly individual and novel creations. The very heterogeneity of Jamaican religion reflects something of the conviction which individuals have about their own special selection by the Holy Spirit for particular inspiration and propheticism. The membership percentages for the main denominations for the years 1960 and 1970 are shown below. It will be seen that there is some obvious falling-off of numbers in the more conventional forms of Christianity, such as Anglicans, Baptists, Methodists and Moravians. During the past decade, however, the incidence of American-inspired Pentecostal, Seventh-Day Adventist and Revivalist churches generally has increased considerably. There is also a tendency for the middle and upper classes to pursue more conventional forms of religion, whilst the lower classes tend to follow the more emotional and less constricting forms.

Between the census of 1943 and that of 1970 the proportion of Anglicans fell drastically from 28.3 per cent to 15.4 per cent whilst that of Roman Catholics rose from 5.7 to 7.9 per cent. There are some signs that the Anglican Church lost prestige after the Declaration of Independence in 1962, and that it is more than probable that the percentage of Anglican members has declined even further. It should also be noted that today the United Church of Jamaica and Grand Cayman represents the union of a large number of the Presbyterian and Congregationalist churches.

Jamaica is proud of its ecumenism. Its ecumenical movement is generally regarded as being well in advance of similar movements in both developed and developing countries. One of the manifestations of interdenominational cooperation in the islands is the Jamaican Council of Churches, which came into being on 10 July, 1941. On that day representatives of ten branches of the Christian Church formally accepted the aims and constitution of the Council. This action paved the way for some meaningful

Jamaican Religious Statistics

	Percentage of Total Population	
Denomination	1960	1970
Anglican	19.7	15.4
Baptist	19.0	17.8
Church of God	11.9	17.0
Roman Catholic	7.2	7.9
Methodist	6.8	6.0
Presbyterian	5.1	5.2
Seventh-Day Adventist	4.9	6.5
Moravian	3.2	2.9
Congregationalist	1.4	*
Pentecostalist	0.9	3.2
Plymouth Brethren	0.9	1.8
Salvation Army	0.6	
Society of Friends	0.2	
Others	18.1	16.3

* Included in Presbyterian
Source: *Statistical Yearbook of Jamaica* 1977

dialogue between all the main Christian communities on the island, and it benefited both the Church as a whole and the country at large.

The main objectives of the Council are firstly, to provide a means whereby all Christian bodies in Jamaica can act together; secondly, to study the problems and opportunities which challenge the Christian way of life; thirdly, to promote, wherever possible, co-operative action; fourthly, to make it clear by public statements the sort of spiritual issues which face the nation; and fifthly, to provide a means of communication with similar councils elsewhere. The following are currently members of the Jamaican Council of Churches:

African Methodist Episcopal Church
Anglican Church
Church of God in Jamaica
Jamaica Baptist Union
Methodist Church
Moravian Church
Roman Catholic Church
Salvation Army
Society of Friends
United Church of Jamaica and Grand Cayman

There have been a number of co-operative ventures which affect the internal dynamics of the various churches themselves. For some time, for example, the churches have been collaborating, on both a national and regional basis, in producing hymn books, modernizing church music, and ceremony, and in teaching religious education.

It would seem clear that in Jamaica ecumenism has already proved workable and meaningful to the society at large. In order to organize the movement fully for both survival and further propagation, the Christian community in Jamaica and the West Indies has committed itself to an important training venture, namely, the United Theological College. At a meeting held in May 1964, eleven Christian denominations agreed that for the purpose of training their ministers they would establish this United Theological College close to the University of the West Indies, and that they would maintain it.

In 1965 a union was formed between the Presbyterians and the Congregationalists and the product was called the United Church of Jamaica and Grand Cayman. This Church has for some years been having discussions with the Moravians and the Disciples of Christ with a view to extending the already existing bond of fellowship. Similar discussions for a union between Anglican and Methodist communities have also been taking place. In general, cooperation between the churches in Jamaica has produced some worthwhile projects, such as Operation Friendship, an organization which provides services ranging from childcare facilities to medical care, and seeks to train people of all age groups in basic literacy and technical skills. The Jamaican Council of Churches also organizes advisory bureaux for citizens, dealing with all types of problems. At the request of the Council, the Ethiopian Orthodox Church was officially established in Jamaica by the Archimandrite Abba Laike Mandefro, the Ethiopian-born head and administrator of the Ethiopian Orthodox Church in the United States. This occurred in May 1970 on the occasion of the Archimandrite's first visit to Jamaica. One or two small groups in the western part of Kingston had previously held services in line with the ritual of the Ethiopian Orthodox Church, indicating their desire to maintain a link with Ethiopia at the Christian level.

During the Archimandrite's first visit 750 new members were baptized, 600 at Kingston Parish Church and 150 at the Ebenezer Church in Western Kingston. Branches of the Church have since been set up in St Thomas and Montego Bay, and the total Jamaican membership now exceeds 2,000. As an illustration of the active ecumenism of Jamaica it is interesting to note that the first services of the Ethiopian Orthodox Church were held in Anglican, Methodist and other church halls. Moreover, the Governor General launched a fund on 1 September, 1971, to assist members of the Community to acquire and establish their own community centre. During the same month the Kingston and St Andrew Corporation passed a resolution which authorized the long-term lease of one acre of the Corporation's land to the Ethiopian Orthodox Church, for the establishment of a community complex, to be used for youth activities and workshops.

In this government and local support of the Ethiopian Orthodox Church one can see not only an extension of the strong ecumenism of the Jamaican society, but also an attempt to strengthen their links with Africa, and with Ethiopia in particular. It is, moreover, an alliance at the more conventional and established Christian level, as distinct from the non-Christian Rastafarian attachment. It provides a positive and functional haven for those Jamaicans who wish to assert strongly their African origins, yet have no great desire to emigrate to Africa, but are anxious rather to do something of a constructive nature in their society.

In Jamaica about 17 per cent of the population do not claim to have any particular religious belief; these are regarded by the rest as free-thinkers. It is generally considered essential to 'belong' to some group or other, and the majority of people attend church services at least once on Sunday and often during the week as well. Church-going is looked upon as a social occasion for which best clothes must be worn, the men in sober suits and the women generally in white dresses and hats.

The church is often a centre of social activity in addition to making provision for worship; thus, for example, the church frequently organizes clubs and holidays for young people. In more general terms, as far as the local community is concerned the church serves as an agency of communication; public notices, instructions and even local gossip are given during the service. Even such routine matters as the necessity for parents to make arrangements for their children's enrolment at school are mentioned. In addition to all these functions the provisions made by church halls include cooking, serving meals, arranging sleeping facilities and organizing basic schools.

In general the various religious organizations reflect quite closely the social structure of the community. The many and varied sects meet the social and psychological, as well as the more religious and pneumatological, needs of the mass of the people, providing emotional excitement, reassurance and release from their sense of oppression. Further, membership of and status within a particular congregation provides the individual with a social identity in the wider community, in which ministers and lay officials enjoy particular prestige. And although there is evidence that there is some falling-off in attendance by young people, church membership is still a very important factor in the social life of the majority of Jamaicans.

In terms of social class the wealthier middle classes of mixed colour tend to belong to the more orthodox churches, and particularly the Anglican Church. Most of the Chinese who are Christian attend Roman Catholic churches. The reason for this appears to be that at the turn of the century most of the Chinese children in Jamaica received their education in Roman Catholic schools, so it normally followed that when they embraced Christianity they joined that church. In addition to this, the Roman Catholic Church in Jamaica has maintained a Chinese Catholic Action Association since about 1930. There are, of course, Chinese Jamaicans who belong to other denominations, and a small minority of older Chinese who are not Christians.

The black lower classes tend to be members of the native, cult and sectarian groups such as the Seventh Day Adventist Churches, the Pentecostals and the great variety of the Churches of God. The Seventh Day Adventists are strongly opposed to the use of drugs, including tea, coffee, tobacco and all alcoholic beverages. They have, in fact, promoted an active programme to assist people who wish to stop smoking; and they continually emphasize that a strong body contributes to spiritual and mental well-being. Adventists observe Saturday as the true sabbath and they believe in the imminent Second Coming (or Advent) of Christ. Whilst not presuming to predict precise dates – they have learned too many lessons from the past – they believe that the 'signs of the times' are increasing in number and that the divine event is not too far off. When Jesus finally returns to earth he will take up his followers to heaven for a thousand years and will leave sinners to burn up along with the devil. Only then will the Kingdom of Heaven be established upon earth.

Religious ideas and principles are used to reinforce social and political purposes. Thus, on radio programmes concerned with family planning, religious faith is invoked through such catchphrases as 'Family Planning is God's Way'. Other radio programmes deal with problems of a specifically religious and moral nature; thus on two evenings a week a programme called 'Can we help you?' goes on the air. In this some attempt is made to deal with questions of conscience.

Of all the American movements which have developed in Jamaica the Pentecostal sects have held a particular appeal, and the Pentecostal Church of the Nazarene was formed in 1907 in an attempt to link the many ramifications of Pentecostalism. The Pentecostal churches are referred to by a variety of names, such as the Elimites, the Assemblies of God, the Apostolic churches and even the Holy Rollers. The members of this Church believe that they are specially holy and chosen by God, and that the Holy Spirit endows them with glossolalia, the gift of tongues. The Church itself is the mystic 'Bride of Christ', but each individual member is responsible for his own soul and his own purity. Because of this individual responsibility, there is in each Pentecostal sect what M. Calley has referred to as an 'endemic heresy'. Each leader feels that he has been selected by God to lead his group or congregation into spiritual unity, in preparation for the coming of Christ. The rites of the Pentecostals include baptism by immersion and holy communion, which is to them the equivalent of the Agape or love-feast of the early Christian Church.

In addition to the Pentecostal churches themselves there is a general Pentecostal movement which has entered a great many of the Nonconformist sects. Since the mid-1950s, and due very much to North American influences, Neo-Pentecostalism has affected the attitude of many Christians towards the gifts of the Spirit, and in particular that of speaking with tongues. There has been a great deal of controversy about the real nature of glossolalia, as to whether it is ecstatic speech, gibberish, inspired utterances in foreign tongues, heavenly language and so forth. One view is that though glossolalia is not gibberish it is not made up of natural languages; another view, after an examination of taped Pentecostalist sessions, is that there exists no correlation at all between the actual glossolalia and the interpretations given.

The Pentecostalists believe, however, that through glossolalia, irrespective of any spiritual significance which the actual words may have, their spirits are strengthened, and they are abandoned completely to the control of something (or Someone) beyond the individual self. In psychological terms this produces in them a sense of euphoria; in spiritual terms they believe that they have been inspired to make utterances which may, or may not, be interpreted, but which indicate to them that the Holy Spirit is working through them. In order that the Spirit may have full control it is essential that their lives are pure, that all illicit forms of sexual intercourse are eschewed, that they do not wear jewellery, straighten their hair, drink alcoholic liquor, smoke, go to cinemas, or swear.

Although there is an essential unity of purpose and identity of ritual behaviour among Pentecostalists, individuals may feel suddenly inspired or elected to begin a new group with some novel ritual or doctrine. The name Holy Rollers was first attached to some Pentecostal groups in America because of some of the phenomena which resulted from their ecstasy – they shouted, twitched, danced, clapped and rolled on the ground. Most of the Pentecostal groups believe in complete abandonment to the possession principle; they are being possessed and controlled, and the Spirit 'bloweth where it listeth'.

The present multiplicity of Christian sects and denominations in Jamaica is but an example of the proselytizing zeal of the many people who firmly believe that they, and they alone, have the right presentation of the truth. Like most of the other disparate sects in Jamaica, the Church of God originated in the United States of America. It was founded as a Baptist denomination in 1830 by John Winebrenner; today, however, there are many varieties of the Church of God to be found both in America and in Jamaica. One particular sect began to take form in the USA in the 1880s, largely through the music, writing and evangelistic preaching of a group of gospel workers. This sect established its headquarters at Anderson, Indiana in 1906 and today it has some 2,250 congregations throughout the USA. In 1907 they started work in Jamaica where there are now over eighty-five congregations. Like a lot of other sects, the Church of God (Anderson) began as a reawakening of a sense of holiness coupled with a burning desire for personal righteousness and the unity of all Christians.

Through its missions the Church of God has spread widely throughout the Caribbean. It is a movement in the Wesleyan tradition in which its followers seek for a special infilling of the Holy Spirit after their conversion, and aim to grow in the Spirit. There is no specific ceremony for joining the Church and no formal membership-rolls are kept. They assert that they regard any Christian anywhere as a member of God's church; any genuine Christian who worships with a local Church of God congregation is a member of God's one church, and they have no other requirement. Because they have no stated creed or discipline a great diversity has developed in the various Churches of God. Each local congregation in Jamaica directs its own affairs, calls its own minister, and decides on its own ways of co-operating to get work done beyond its borders. There is a great deal of emphasis upon the Bible and its verbal inspiration, and the general theological position is a conservative and evangelical one, with emphasis upon the Trinity, and upon Christ as their Lord and Saviour.

The Church of God seeks to educate its people for full citizenship in the Body of Christ, the Church. Man is God's supreme creation and through Christ as Saviour he seeks to return to God from whom he has strayed. At the 'end of the age' Christ will return for his millennial reign upon the earth with his faithful followers. Whilst the Church of God in Jamaica is not committed to speaking in tongues, there are certainly many congregations who do get involved in ecstasy, dissociation, and in some instances speaking with tongues. Most Churches of God, however, are involved in other 'gifts of the Spirit' such as spiritual healing. The whole idea of spiritual healing is strongly held throughout Jamaica, from the animistic levels of obeah and pocomania to the Christian concept of mediation of the Holy Spirit. Members of the Church of God usually accept the rituals of baptism by immersion, foot washing of full church members, and the commemoration of the Lord's Supper.

The great variety of churches in Jamaica help, between them, to fulfil the religious, cultural and social needs of the people. Religion plays an important part in the great proportion of the lives of the majority of Jamaicans; and although the church no longer holds a uniquely influential position in the community, because of the development of popular education and the mass media, it still represents a social and cohesive force in the country. This is particularly true of the rural districts. In religious terms the churches provide an emotional release, and involvement in the services is spontaneous and often total. This applies mainly to the popular religious sects in which the congregational responses are simple, repetitive and virtually continuous. In cultural terms, whilst in some areas the church represents a very vital and vigorous force, in other areas this side is completely overlooked. In social terms, some established religious groups cater for those people in the community who already have most status as well as providing a social outlet and some status for those who have none. Local community leaders tend to figure prominently at church services, since prominence in a church gives prestige within the community of that church. Sects such as the Pentecostal, the Seventh Day Adventist and the Church of God have a greater appeal for the simpler, poorer people because of the emphasis they place upon salvation. In the realm of religion even the poorest find some sense of equality.

The ministers of all the churches exert a strong influence on the community, and this applies to both the more orthodox types of church and the Pentecostal and evangelical sects generally. Women ministers also have considerable influence as balm-women with special healing powers. The churches, too, are concerned with the main rituals of life – its *rites de passage* – with birth, conversion, baptism, marriage and death. The baptism of infants varies according to the rites of each religious denomination, but there is still a superstitious concern regarding the protection of the child at birth. The first eight days after birth are considered to be highly dangerous, and great care must be taken to ward off all evil duppies. Weddings are also very important social events – for those who can afford them – however rare they might be. The average age at marriage is 31.7 years for brides and 36.0 years for bridegrooms, whilst the rate of illegitimacy still remains at 70 per cent.

In addition to everything that has been said about the function of the church in Jamaica in its manifold forms, perhaps its most profound role is its therapeutic and cathartic one. The rhythms, the responses, the hand-clapping and foot-beating, the swaying and shouting, the dissociation, trance state and its self-hypnotic effect – all these act as a therapy to those who feel that life for them is without hope or the possibility of resolution. Through the emotional appeal of the sermons, which stress a better life to come and a revivalist approach to present conditions, many find peace and comfort.

Chapter 13
Religion and Jamaican Society

We have seen that there remain in Jamaica certain elements of African religion, taken over as a racial and cultural inheritance. There are also interesting revivalist cults which provide an infusion of fresh enthusiasm and hope; and there are elements, such as the Rastafarian, which have political, economic and social implications as well as religious. In addition to Christian sects and denominations there are also groups of people who follow the religions of Hinduism and Judaism.

When slavery had been abolished several unsuccessful attempts were made to replace the slave labour force with European and Chinese workers, and then, beginning in 1845, indentured labourers were introduced from India. The religious background of the latter was either Hindu or Muslim, and as far as possible they remained together and practised their own forms of worship. Some returned home when their contracts had expired, but many remained and became absorbed into the cultural and educational life of the island.

Since there is at present no Hindu temple in Jamaica the Hindus perform their religious ceremonies and ritual in their own homes. Hindu marriages usually take place at the bride's residence. There are two established mosques in Jamaica, one in St Catherine and the other in Westmoreland.

Until 1959 every descendant of an indentured labourer from India was labelled an immigrant. Indians had to obtain a 'certificate of no impediment' from the official assigned to the protection of immigrants before a legally valid marriage could be performed, and marriages performed according to Hindu rites were not recognized. In such cases, when a man died intestate everything that belonged to him was administered by the government, since he was presumed not to have any lawful heirs. Nothing was awarded to the widow and children because they were considered to be illegitimate. In order to escape this fate many Hindus married in a Christian church or in the office of the Civil Registrar of Marriages. As a result, however, of the strong representations made by the East Indian Progressive Society, the Jamaican government now recognizes marriages performed by the marriage officers of both Hinduism and Islam.

We mentioned earlier the fact that Jews from Spain and Portugal settled in Jamaica, usually as refugees from the Spanish Inquisition. After the occupation by the British in 1655 the Jews openly practised their religion. During the ensuing years other groups of Jews entered Jamaica from Germany and Central Europe. In the early days they formed separate congregations, but during the present century the various congregations merged to form The United Congregation of Israelites.

The various churches in Jamaica have made an outstanding contribution to the educational development of their society. All legal barriers to the education of black Jamaicans were removed after emancipation, and the churches grasped every opportunity offered, when a church or meeting house was erected, to build a school. Both primary and secondary schools originated in the church; many schools were sponsored by the various denominations, and in fact the majority of the trusts which were established for charitable and educational purposes arose out of religious inspiration. Most of such schools have survived, and at the present time the Church as an institution is responsible in some way for about 75 per cent of the high schools in Jamaica. Most of the existing teachers' training colleges have also been founded by some branch of the Christian church, the first in the field being the Moravians. Although, since the turn of the century, the government has increasingly assumed the responsibility for the education of the population, there still exists a great deal of participation by the Church in education, with considerable co-operation and understanding at all levels.

In most parts of Jamaica influential leaders tend to be involved in local or national politics or are important in the churches. There is still a strong tendency for people to turn to the local minister and/or teacher for practical help and advice. Both teachers and ministers are natural leaders in Jamaica because of the central importance of both religion and education in their community, and because of the authority that is still largely vested in them.

Weddings, baptisms and funerals are, as we have seen, important occasions which sometimes bring together all the members of a particular village or community. The churches themselves provide a meeting place for a great many people pursuing a variety of hobbies or skills. Christian marriage still tends to be the ideal rather than the realized: it is a middle-class practice requiring middle-class capital; common law marriage is prevalent at the lower economic levels.

Whilst this position is generally accepted, among the more keenly religious a Christian marriage would be preferred.

The churches, at least, some of them, are involved in family-planning advice, voluntary social work, basic schools, literacy schemes and the care of the sick. There is an increasing tendency for the churches to go out into society and help people in their present situation, rather than to insist upon the importance of regular church-attendance. There is a developing awareness of the part the church has to play in the total life of the community.

In order to put the various types of religious sects into some perspective it may be useful to view them in a classified form. B.R. Wilson has provided us with a typology, and this may well serve as a means of relating the many sects, denominations and cults which are to be found in Jamaica, and also of viewing the way in which they interrelate with their society. These types, of course, are not mutually exclusive; some Christian sects clearly straddle, in their characteristics, two or more of the classes indicated. This is simply a reflection of the fact that religion, like most social phenomena, is not amenable to precise description or classification. In religion, in particular, there is always the element of the surd, the irrational, or perhaps more accurately the non-rational – that which is not reducible to any precise scientific or sociological analysis. The types are (1) conversionist, (2) revolutionary, (3) introversionist, (4) manipulationist, (5) thaumaturgical, (6) reformist, and (7) utopian.

The *conversionist* type of religion or sect, in terms of Christianity, derives largely from a fundamentalist or literalist approach to the Christian scriptures. Man is a fallen creature; created perfect, he ate of the forbidden fruit of knowledge and so became sinful. Moreover, his sin and guilt are passed on from one generation to another so that both man and society have become thoroughly corrupted. Both man and society, however, can be transformed through man's personal redemption. This is an evangelical approach to religion which seeks to proselytize the individual and the masses through an emotional appeal to the sense of guilt and the awareness of the need for salvation. The possibility of salvation has been provided by a saviour, a divine being, who has come to earth in human form specifically for the purpose of man's redemption.

The meetings of these conversionist groups arouse strong emotional reactions and practices, which may not begin by being ecstatic but which, in many instances, cease to be self-controlled and eventually become other-controlled. It is important in this type of religion to accept any doctrines which are propounded even though they may not be completely understood; the individual will 'feel through' to their inner meaning, and rational comprehension becomes relatively unimportant. Conversionist religion, as such, is not primarily concerned with social programmes of reform, but with the reformation, or conversion, of the individual.

In Jamaica this particular type of sect covers a considerable number of groups, including the Salvation Army, a large number of Assemblies of God and Churches of God, as well as a variety of Pentecostal movements. In addition, there are many individual gospel missions (such as the 'Light House Full Gospel of God') and halls (such as the 'Mount Carmel Gospel Hall') that aim at conversion. These include also a variety of Baptist evangelistic chapels.

It is perhaps significant that in recent years a number of these conversionist sects, or at least individual leaders of such sects, have involved themselves in a variety of social activities, including the provision of youth clubs, basic schools, literacy schemes, sewing classes and so forth to help the transformation of society itself in however small a way.

The *revolutionary* type of sect relates to the total social position and it is likely to arise in a situation which is largely dysnomic, and in which the people are depressed and suffering from poverty, unemployment and political exploitation. Religious movements and sects which are born in this sort of social soil are often revolutionary and eschatological; that is, they rebel against the present social order and seek to set up, 'at the end of the age', 'at the end of time', or 'in the last days', a new order under God himself. These movements are not in the least interested in social reform through human endeavour or in political action. Man, in their view, is quite incapable by himself of achieving any sort of reform either in his own nature or in society. God has had a plan since before the beginning of time, and all earthly life and action are predetermined by that divine plan. In this plan there is no opportunity for individual human freedom, and so sudden or instantaneous conversion tends to be frowned upon; such conversion, for this type at least, would seem to imply too much individual freewill to make a personal and immediate decision. Conversion, thus, is a gradual process produced by a form of continuous indoctrination until the inevitable becomes an actuality.

In the revolutionary sect there is generally far less emphasis upon moral behaviour than in the conversionist sect, but there is a great proclivity towards prophecy, prophetic signs and their interpretation. As far as Christianity is concerned there will be in such a sect a great deal of emphasis on the Old Testament prophets as well as on the Book of Revelation. Examination of these sources inevitably leads to some precise predictions as to the time of the 'Latter Days' and millennial expectancy. God is their leader and dictator and he reveals himself and his eschatological message to his true believers and followers. Amongst such revolutionary groups in Jamaica is the well-known Christian sect of Jehovah's Witnesses, or the Watchtower Bible and Tract Society, sometimes referred to as the Church of the Latter Day Saints. They have, however, no great following there.

The Rastafarians, whether Christian or not, certainly correspond very closely to the revolutionary type. They consider that their God, Jehovah, has ordained a time when, through his chosen instruments, he will fulfil the Biblical prophecies and promises concerning the lost children of the house of Israel. Led by their messiah-saviour, the Negus, they will enter the black promised land of Ethiopia; whilst the white Babylon, with all its imperialism, racialism and evil, will be destroyed for ever. No sect, or group of sects, represents more closely the adventist expectation, the millenarian hope and the Chiliastic doctrines of some of the earlier forms of Christianity than the Rastafarians. There is for them no hope in society itself; nor is there any possibility of its transformation through human agency alone; only the Messiah can alter the world situation and reverse the position of slaves and masters as it exists today.

The *introversionist* type of sect neither seeks to convert the world, nor expects any ultimate eschatological overturn of society. Because it regards the world and society as irredeemable, it aims simply to retire from the world into a state of perfect holiness. Social reforms may take place, individuals may be converted to this or that, and society may be in a state of revolution, but for the introversionist sect these things are of little moment. God, in his wisdom, love and preordination, has chosen his vessels for honour, and he will pour out his Holy Spirit upon them. Such vessels are destined to fulfil his will and purpose for them by being pure and holy in his sight, by reading the Scriptures, and by listening for and accepting the Spirit's inspired interpretation. These 'holy ones' represent God's chosen remnant who will eventually be called by God to do his purpose.

There have been holiness movements in Jamaica since about 1919 when the Darbyists, or Plymouth Brethren, first established their church there. The Plymouth Brethren sect was founded in 1827 by John Darby, a minister of the Church of Ireland, and Edward Cronin, a former Roman Catholic. They had felt some dissatisfaction with the lack of spirituality and holiness in their own churches, so they joined forces and held small meetings with breaking of bread every Sunday in Dublin. Darby eventually settled in Plymouth, which gave his supporters the name of Plymouth Brethren. There followed many splinter groups of the Brethren – the Exclusives, the Newtonites, the Kellyites and Bethesda. They disagreed on such things as church government and the endowments or powers of the Holy Spirit. The Open Brethren have made the sacraments open to all believers, as distinct from the Exclusive Brethren who will have no truck with unbelievers, or those who depart in any way from their specific beliefs; this rule applies equally to unbelievers within their own family.

In addition to the Plymouth Brethren in Jamaica the holiness sects are represented chiefly by the Calvary Holiness Church, the First Church of the Apostolic Faith, the Holiness Christian Church Inc., the Pilgrim Holiness Church, and the United Holy Church of God. On the whole, however, it is true to say that such introversionist types of religion do not have a great deal of success among a people who in general are extrovert in their beliefs and behaviour. The Jamaicans are an outgoing and generous people and they do care about others within their society, so that any sectarian belief which tends to exclude all others, both religiously and socially, is regarded with a great deal of suspicion.

The *manipulationist* sects claim to have particular and peculiar knowledge which empowers them to manipulate the forces of nature. In general terms, these sects and cults are a development of the Gnostic principle that there is a body of knowledge waiting to be revealed to those who are ready to receive it, and who will thereby become initiates into the secrets of the Universe. Most Gnostic cults, although not insisting upon any body of doctrine to be believed by their members, do accept that there is a divinity, however described, who is the source and basis for all the laws and principles of the universe, especially the spiritual order or dimension. Such manipulationist sects and cults exist to develop special techniques for the conquest of both natural and spiritual realms. They are syncretistic in that they accept the principle that 'truth is where you find it', and their beliefs tend to form a pastiche of all that they consider valuable in their desire to subdue the forces that appear to control and determine man.

The manipulationist is mainly concerned with the here and now and with self-development in present time. But this does not derive from any lack of interest in what is popularly termed the after-life. Rather it is elicited from a total philosophy of time and eternity which views the spiritual dimension as being outside linear time altogether. In this spiritual dimension one lives perpetually in eternity, and death itself is simply an incident in the totality of existence. This explains the lack of interest shown in the prophetic and eschatological elements of religion.

Christian Science, as a manipulationist sect, has only a small following in Jamaica, and, in fact, there is very little development of what might be termed the more Gnostic movements, such as Rosicrucianism or the Martinists. These developments represent a sophistication of religion which has found very little response at any level of Jamaican society. There are, however, manipulationist elements in the forms of magic or pseudo-magic which have a nativistic origin. It is here that, in Jamaica at any rate, the manipulationist and the thaumaturgical types of religion overlap.

The *thaumaturgical* sects accept that their members, or at least some of them, are miracle-makers or wonder-workers and that the lives of all members are affected by such spiritual activities. The wonder-workers are themselves manipulationists; they manipulate nature and use the powers of the spiritual universe to attain their ends. Whilst the true manipulationist is not concerned with the trivia of life, but with the universal principles behind all phenomena, the thaumaturge is interested in the great variety of paranormal activity at every level. The thaumaturge may not understand his powers; indeed, he may not even be concerned to understand them so long as they work. He may not make any special claim or have any special gnosis, but he can 'call spirits from the vasty deep', heal, speak in tongues, bring injury upon his enemies and upon the enemies of others.

Among the thaumaturgical sects in Jamaica there are various spiritualist churches which conduct seances, perform cures, and link the people with their ancestors. But in addition to the more orthodox spiritualist churches there are the nativistic cults which link what we are pleased to call pagan religious elements with Christian elements. The Pocomania sects are, generally speaking, a thaumaturgic syncretism of pagan and Christian practices; whilst Obeah is a thaumaturgical cult at the nativistic level. There are, however, many of the Christian church members who have some acceptance of the practices of obeah, or myal, and who on occasion make use of them. The thaumaturgical element is very strong indeed in the great variety of Christian sects and groups in Jamaica, and this is particularly noticeable in sects with some sort of African title or affiliation.

The *reformist* type of sect in Jamaica is represented by the Religious Society of Friends, or Quakers, which has a small following. Doctrines are of minimal importance in this type, whilst the humanitarian element is maximized. The aim of such sects is to transform society and the relationship between people, to arouse and develop the social conscience, and to have concern for the world and its problems whilst retaining a personal integrity and 'keeping oneself unspotted from the world'. It has a certain 'holiness' attitude without any desire to withdraw completely from the world itself. The present movement of the *International Peacemakers' Association,* started by Claudius Henry, although nominally Rastafarian and possessing something of the millenarian concept, is to a very large extent reformist in that Henry and his followers are concerned with the immediate reformation of their own society and with its extension. It is a thoroughly humanitarian movement which has gradually increased its concern for people here and now. They are no longer anxious for any return of the lost tribes to the Ethiopian promised land, but rather keen to improve the lot of all the Jamaicans who come under their influence, in terms of their physical, social and educational requirements as well as their spiritual needs.

B.R. Wilson has said of the *utopian* type of sect that 'it is more radical than the reformist sect, potentially less violent than the revolutionary sect and more constructive on a social level than the conversionist sect'. The utopian sect does not withdraw entirely from the outside world, but sees its function as one of seeking to know and understand fully the existing world in order to reshape it and make it a better place. This it hopes to do not so much in terms of a utopia unrelated to anything known and observed, as in terms of the real, living situation of people's immediate needs. In Jamaica this type of sect is not represented by any particular group or denomination, although inevitably there are those in most sects who become involved in some way in communal living with an ideal such as that possessed by the early Christian church.

Many Jamaicans, of course, as we have already seen, seek their utopia in their African ancestral home; but many more have collective visions and experiences of an ecstatic nature in which their ultimate sense of identity and belonging are evoked, and in which they find their eschatological hopes revealed and fulfilled. The possession syndrome releases them into a world that they feel they have known in the past and that they would wish to know again; a world which is peculiarly theirs, with their own belief, cult, rites and culture; a black culture, a black religion, a black life. Some are unable to see any development of their society in any sort of modem context. Some, such as the Rastafarians, have become dysnomic in their attitudes because they cannot see the possibility of change within their society, or any hope of betterment. Others look forward to the creation of a new culture which will develop naturally out of the needs of specific economic, political and social situations, supported by religious forms which are directly related to their spiritual insights.

Chapter 14
Conclusion

Religion and religious life are of importance to the great majority of the Jamaican people. The richness and variety of religious beliefs and adherence are an indication that the spiritual dimension forms a vital aspect of Jamaican life and culture. Church-going on Sundays is an important event, providing social as well as spiritual identity for the participants. But religion spills over into everyday life in a variety of ways: daily radio broadcasts express proselytizing zeal and fervour; numerous meetings are held during the week, some of which may well last up to five or more hours, providing considerable excitement, noise and physical activity; morning assemblies and religious education in the schools are intended to promote a unity and identity of purpose among the young. In the main religion is a joyous activity and most of the religious celebrations of the Jamaicans express a warmth and friendliness second to none. With the exception of the few exclusive sects, they welcome the visitor in their midst and all may participate freely in the services. This goes further than a mere tolerance of a stranger; it is a genuine feeling and experience of identity with all who have come to worship.

There is also a strong correlation between the socioeconomic status of the individual Jamaican and the sort of religious group or sect to which he belongs. The upper and middle classes tend to gravitate towards the more orthodox denominational churches, such as the Anglican, the Roman Catholic, Methodist and Presbyterian. The lower classes, on the whole, seem, to prefer the Church of God, the Pentecostal sects and the various cult groups. The Rastafarians embrace a wide variety of individuals from all levels of society, from the politically and socially disaffected drop-outs to the sophisticated and highly intelligent potential leaders of revolt. But to most Jamaicans religion represents a mode of withdrawing from the somewhat hopeless social and economic deprivation that they suffer into the compensatory warmth and fellowship of the small chapel hall or the larger church assembly.

When the Jamaican leaves his homeland and comes to Britain he quickly becomes aware of a society which is motivated by vastly different purposes, hopes and ambitions. Firstly, it is a society which is considerably more technological and sophisticated than his own, one which is orientated towards economic success, and in which to most members of society the acquisition of wealth and possessions is vastly more important than the development of spirituality. Indeed, he finds a society whose culture has become secular and in which there is a considerable decline in the attendance of church and in the practice of religion at all social levels.

A number of studies have been conducted in Britain during the past decade or so in order to enquire into the effect of our western ideas and culture upon immigrants who have settled here, and a certain general pattern seems to emerge. Obviously those immigrants who have lived longest in Britain tend to be the most greatly affected by secularism and materialism. As their social ambitions have increased so their interest in church and religion has tended to decrease. Many West Indians have also said quite clearly that they have found it virtually impossible to participate in the services of white churches. They have found the churches cold, unfriendly, unemotional and distant. In consequence, they have ceased going to church or, in some instances, have developed their own separate and segregated churches and congregations. The continuous vocal response demanded by the congregation throughout some of the Jamaican church services, for example, is quite alien to the more reserved English nature and character. And so acculturation in our society has meant for many a complete rejection or abandonment of religious observance, or at least an ever decreasing attachment to religion, whilst the young, who are affected almost *ab initio* by our social attitudes and mores, rebel vigorously against any relics of Jamaican compulsion in church attendance.

In his study of 'Some Aspects of Religious Life in an Immigrant Area in Manchester', Robin H. Ward has this to say about some coloured families opting out of church-going altogether:

> Coming from a high status background in the West Indies to a position of disprivilege in Moss Side, they can either join a respectable white church which is unlikely to accept them fully, and which legitimates a style of life they do not fully share, or they can become attached to a low status, probably West Indian church, which they had previously looked down on, but which will provide support against and compensation for the damage to their self-image which they suffer in British society. In face of this it may be surprising that the white denominations have received so many West Indians into their churches.

Those Jamaican immigrants in Britain who feel totally rejected or deprived tend to group together to form their own Pentecostal groups rather than join indigenous Pentecostal churches. The reason for this is not far to seek. Through their own sense of rejection, they too have rejected everything connected with western society and its values, which they regard, in this instance as wicked and depraved in the extreme. They look forward in their religious affiliation to the millennial period when Christ the Messiah will return in power and glory, to destroy the powers of darkness and to justify the righteous. It is, perhaps, one of the saddest reflections upon the immigration into Britain of West Indian groups that, even though most of their religious sects have at least some connection with Christianity, there is almost complete division from the host society at the religious level. The one factor that might have united has, instead, tended to become divisive, and to set one against another even in the spiritual dimension. One can only hope that the Jamaican motto, 'Out of Many, One People', may have a wider truth in our rapidly developing multi-racial and multicultural society.

Bibliography

Augier, F.R., *et alii*, *The Making of the West Indies* (Longmans, 1960)
Barrett, L.E., *The Rastafarians* (Univ. of Puerto Rica, 1969)
Baxter, Ivy, *The Arts of an Island* (Scarecrow Press, 1970)
Beckwith, Martha, *Black Roadways* (Univ. of North Carolina, 1969)
Black, C.V., *The Story of Jamaica* (Collins, revised ed, 1965)
Blake, Judith, *Family Structure in Jamaica* (Free Press of Glencoe, 1961)
Burns, A., *History of the British West Indies* (Allen & Unwin, 1965)
Calley, M.J.C., *God's People: West Indian Pentecostalist Sects in England* (OUP, 1965)
Carley, M.M., *Jamaica: The Old and the New* (Allen & Unwin, 1963)
Carmichael, Mrs, *Five Years in Trinidad & St Vincent* (Whitaker, 1834)
Cassidy, F.G. & Le Page, R.B., *Dictionary of Jamaican English* (CUP, 1967)
Davidson, B., *The African Past* (Penguin, 1966)
De Lisser, H.G., *White Witch of Rosehall (Benn,* 1969)
Deren, Maya, *Divine Horsemen* (Thames & Hudson, 1963)
Elkins, S.M., *Slavery* (Univ of Chicago, 1968)
Emerick, A.J., *Jamaican Myalism* (Woodstock, 1916)
Etzel Pearcy, G., *The West Indian Scene* (van Nostrand, 1965)
Fage, J.D., *An Introduction to the History of West Africa* (CUP, 1955)
Henriques, F.M., *Jamaica: Land of Wood & Water* (MacGibbon & Kee, 2nd ed 1968)
Herskovits, M.J., *The Myth of the Negro Past* (Harper, 1941)
Hill, C.S., *West Indian Migrants & the London Churches* (OUP, 1963)
Hoetink, H., *The Two Variants of Caribbean Race Relations* (OUP, 1967)
Hurston, Z.N., *Voodoo Gods* (Dent, 1939)
Kerr, Madeline, *Personality & Conflict in Jamaica* (Liverpool Univ, 1952)
Lanternari, V., *The Religions of the Oppressed* (NAL, 1965)
Norris, Katrin, *Jamaica: The Search for an Identity* (OUP, 1962)
Owens, J., *Dread* (Sangsters, 1977)
Parrinder, G., *Religion in Africa* (Penguin, 1969)
Patterson, H.O., *The Children of Sisyphus* (Hutchinson, 1964)
Patterson, Sheila, *Dark Strangers* (Penguin Books, 1965)
Rattray, R.S., *Ashanti* (OUP, 1923)

Rattray, R.S., *Akan-Ashanti Folk-Tales* (OUP, 1930)
Seaga, Edward, *Folk Music of Jamaica*
Sherlock, P.M., *The Aborigines of Jamaica* (Kingston, Jamaica, 1939)
Sherlock, P., *Anansi, the Spider Man* (Macmillan, 1964)
Simpson, G.E., 'Jamaican Revivalist Cults', *Social and Economic Studies* (Kingston, Jamaica, 1956) vol.5, No.4 pp.321-442.
Simpson, G.E., 'The Rastafarian Movement in Jamaica', *Social and Economic Studies* (Kingston, Jamaica, 1956)
Smith, E.W. (ed.), *African Ideas of God* (Edinburgh House, 2nd edition 1961)
Smith, M.G., *The Plural Society in the British West Indies* (Univ. of California Press, 1965)
Smith, M.G. et alii, *The Ras Tafari Movement in Kingston, Jamaica* (Kingston, Jamaica, 1960)
Tannenbaum, F., *Slave and Citizen* (Knopf, N.Y., 1947)
Ward, R.H., 'Some Aspects of Religious Life in an Immigrant Area in Manchester' in Martin, D. & Hill, M. (eds), *A Sociological Yearbook of Religion in Britain 3* (SCM Press, 1970)
Williams, E., *British Historians and the West Indies* (Andre Deutsch, 1966)
Williams, J. J., *Voodoos and Obeahs* (Dial Press, N. Y., 1932)
Williams, J. J., *Psychic Phenomena of Jamaica* (Dial Press, N.Y., 1934)
Wilson, B.R., *Patterns of Sectarianism* (Heinemann, 1967)

Appendix 1
Sects and Denominations

African Methodist Episcopal
African Methodist Episcopal – Zion Church
Anglican
Apostolic Church
Apostolic Church of Christ
Apostolic Church of Jamaica Inc.
Apostolic Faith Mission.
Apostolic Methodist Episcopal Church of Zion
Apostolic Missionary Association of Jamaica
Assemblies of God in Jamaica
Assemblies of the Church of God
Assemblies of the First Born
Assembly of Yahweh
Associated Gospel Assemblies
Baptist
Baptist Assembly of Native Evangelism
Baptist Mid-Mission
Bedwardites
Bible Truth Church of God
Bible Way Mission
Blood Bought Church of God
Brethren Church of God
Calvary Holiness Church
Christian Catholic Church
Christian Church
Christian Missionary Alliance
Christian Mission Limited (Christian Brethren)
Christian Science
Church of Christ
Church of God (Anderson, Indiana, USA)
Church of God and Saints of Christ
Church of God Body of Christ
Church of God Holiness
Church of God in Christ
Church of God in Christ Jesus the Apostle
Church of God in Jamaica
Church of God of Prophecy
Church of God Seventh Day
Church of God Universal
Church of Jamaica
Church of Our Lord Jesus Christ Apostolic

Church of the First Born
Church of the Living God
Church of the Living God Pillar and Ground of Truth
Church of the Open Bible
Disciples of Christ in Jamaica
Ebenezer New Testament Church of God in Jamaica
Elders' Church of God
Elim Church
Emanuel Apostolic United Church of Christ Inc.
Ethiopian Orthodox Church
Evangelical Church of Christ
Faith Bible Baptist Church
First Born Church of God
First Glorious Temple Church of God Apostolic
First Holiness Church of the Apostolic Faith
Four Square Church of Christ
Full Gospel Baptist Association
General Baptist
Glad Tidings Open Baptist Church
Glad Tidings Open Bible Church
Gospel Assembly
Gospel Foundation Church of Jamaica
Grace Missionary Church
Holiness Christian Church Inc.
International Church of Four Square Gospel
Jamaica Baptist Union
Jamaica Christian Fellowship
Jamaica Evangelist Mission
Jamaica Fellowship of Independent Baptists
Jamaica Free Baptist Church Union
Jamaica Mission of Seventh Day Christians
Jamaica Seventh Day Baptist
Jehovah's Witnesses (Watchtower Bible and Tract Society)
Life Line Mission
Light House Full Gospel Church of God
Mennonite Church
Methodist
Missionary Bands of the World
Missionary Church Association
Missionary Church Association in Jamaica
Model Church of God
Moravian Church
Mt Carmel Gospel Hall
Mt Zion Sanctuary Inc.
National Baptist Convention of Jamaica and America
New Apostolic Church

New Covenant Church of God
New Testament Assemblies
New Testament Church
New Testament Church of Christ the Redeemer
New Testament Church of God
Open Bible Standard Churches
Pentecostal Assemblies of the World Inc.
Pentecostal Church of God
Pentecostal Church of the Nazarene
Pentecostal Gospel Temple
Pilgrim Holiness Church
Pilgrim Union Church of God
Plymouth Brethren
Presbyterian
Protestant Reform Churches
Rehoboath Gospel Assembly
Rehoboath Church of God in Christ Jesus, Apostolic, Inc.
Religious Society of Friends (Quaker)
Remnant Churches of God
Rock Cliffe Baptist Mission
Roman Catholic
St John's Trinitarian Baptist
Salvation Army
Sanctified Church of God
Seventh Day Adventist
Seventh Day Christian Congress
Seventh Day Christ Mission Inc.
Seventh Day Church of God Assembly
Seventh Day Pentecostal Church of God
Shiloah Apostolic Church of Jamaica Inc.
United Brethren in Christ
United Church of God of the Reform House of God Inc.
United Church of Jamaica and Grand Cayman Isles
United Church of Presbyterians and Congregationalists
United Holy Church of God
United Pentecostal Church
Unity Organization
Universal Church of the Master
Wayside Bethany Assembly
Zion Evangelistic Fellowship Inc.

Confucianists
Hindus
Jews
Muslims

Appendix 2
West Africa: Some Ethnic Groups

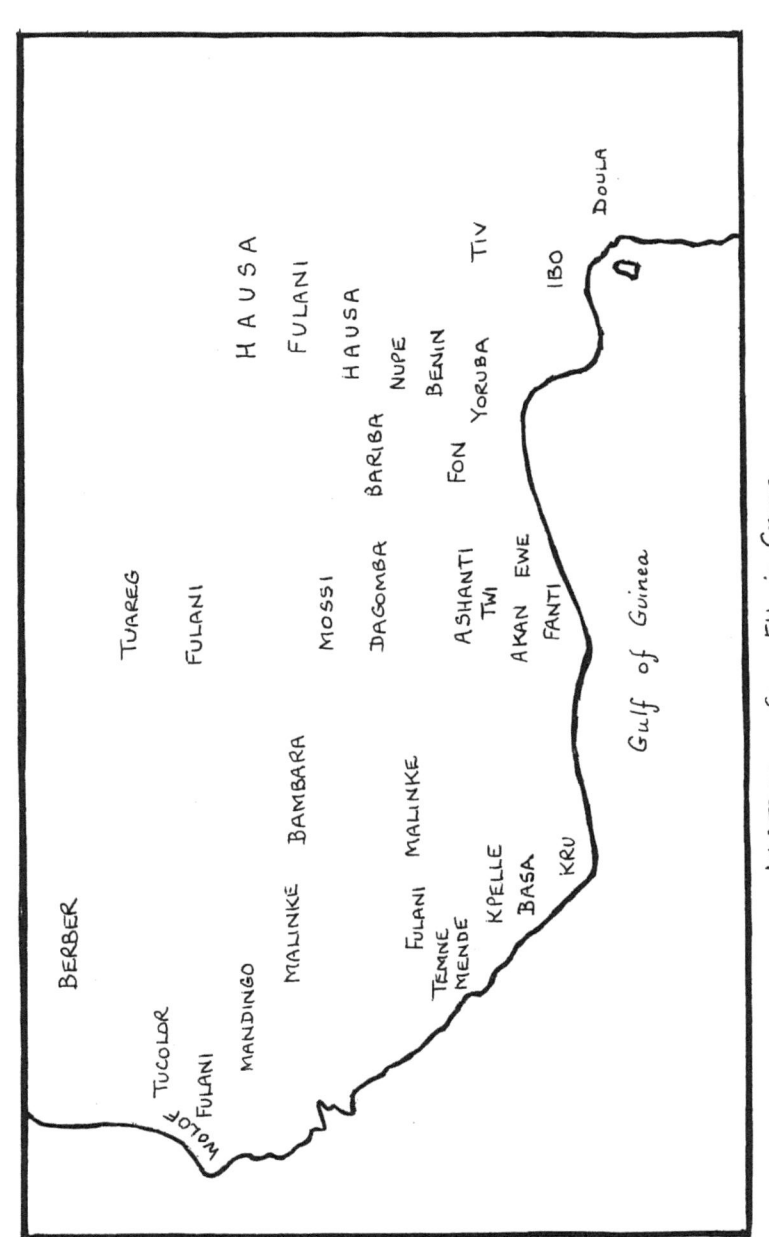

Appendix 3
Jamaica: Parish Boundaries

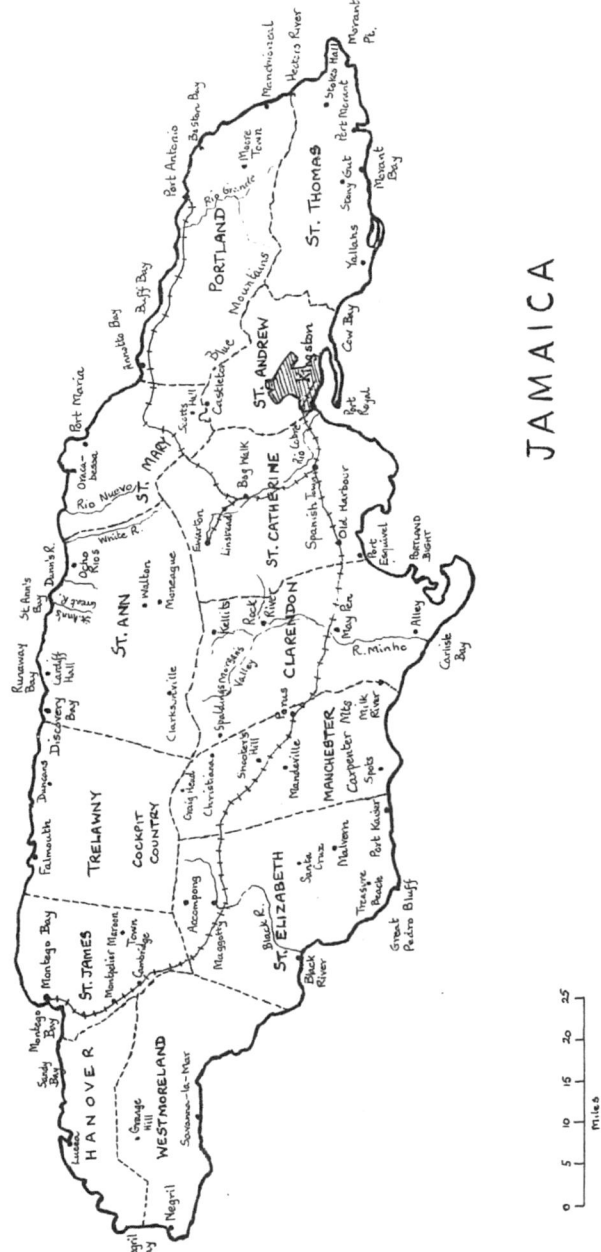

Index

Aborigines 3-8
Abosom 19-21, 46, 55
Accompong 5, 19, 46
Africa 10-24, et passim
African Reform Church 73
Akan-Ashanti 19-21
Anancy-Tacooma folk cycle 43-5
Ananse 21-2
Anglicanism 32-8, 92, 96, 111
Animism 4-8, 17-18
Arawaks 3-8, 32, 49, 59
Ashanti 14-24, 40-8, 65
Assemblies of God 97, 105
Awlawrun 19-20

Babylon 81-90, 106
Back-O-Wall 72-3
Baker, Moses 35, 47
Balm woman 56, 100
Bantu 17
Baptism 100, 103
Baptists 35-7, 92
Beckwith, Maria 52-3
Bedward, Alexander 49-51
Birth control 84
Black power 90-1
Bogle, Paul 38
Brazil 26-8
Brethren 107

Cacique 5
Caribs 3-4
Carmichael, Mrs 25-7, 36, 41
Cassidy, F.G. 13, 45, 59
Caste system 15
Catharsis 20

Celebrations 66-7
Chinese 11-12, 96-7
Christian Science 108
Christian sects 92-101
Church-going 96, 111
Ciboneys 3-4
Coartacion 26
Cockpit country 19, 28, 77
Cohiba 5
Colonial Church Union 37
Columbus, Christopher 3-4, 9
Congregationalists 35, 92
Consolidated Slave Act (1793) 34
Conversionist type 104-5
Creole 16
Cromwell, Oliver 10
Cuba 3f, 9f, 26-8
Cumina 8, 59-62

Dahomey 16, 23, 41
Demon possession 7
Deren, Maya 8
Dialects 16
Disciples of Christ 94
Dreadlocks 72, 83
Dungle 78
Dunkley, Alexander 69-70
Duppies 18, 41-5, 62-4, 100

Ecumenism 92, 95
Elimites 97
Emancipation 37-9
Escapism 84-5
Ethiopia 71-2, 74-6, 80-1, 84, 87-91,
  95, 109
Ethiopian Orthodox Church 76, 80, 95

Ethiopian World Federation Inc 72-3
Exorcism 8, 61

Family planning 84, 97, 104
Fanti 15
Fertility 6, 18, 24, 65
Fetish 7, 23-4, 44-7
Folklore 20-2
Fox, George 34
Fundamentalism 104

Ganja 54, 71, 81, 89
Garvey, Marcus 68
Ghana 15, 76
Glossolalia 48, 53, 97-9
Gnostic cults 107-8
Gold Coast 15-6, 23
Gordon, George William 38
Great Revival 49
Grounation 83

Haile Selasie 69-72, 80-4, 90-1
Haiti 3-4, 8, 11, 23, 27, 41, 53
Hausa 15-6, 20, 30, 33, 45
Henriques, F. 52, 63
Henry, Claudius 73-6, 86-8, 90, 109
Henry, Ronald 75
Hierarchy of Gods 18-20
Hindus 102-3
Holy Rollers 97-8
Howell, Leonard 69-71

Ibos 30
Indians 11, 102-3
Initiation 46
Inquisition 9
International Peacemakers' Association 86-8, 109
Introversionist type 106-7
Islam 15, 33, 103

Jack Mandora 45
Jamaican Council of Churches 92
Jeebis 8
Jehovah's Witnesses 106
John Canoe 64-6
Judaism 102

Kikongo 61
Kingston 68, 72
Koromantyns 16, 19, 23, 28-30, 41
Kumona 8, 52, 59-62

Lanternari, V. 56
Le Page, R.B. 13, 59
Liberia 68, 76
Lisle, G. 35, 47
Loa 53
Locksmen 71, 83

Magic 22-4
Mana 7, 17
Manipulationist type 107-8
Manitu 17
Manumission 26
Maroons 5, 10-11, 16, 19, 28, 59
Marriage 30, 66-7, 103
Masai 72
Messianism 51, 68-70, 73-4, 84-7, 113
Methodism 36, 47, 49-50, 111
Millenarianism 89, 99, 106, 109, 113
Mmotia 17, 44
Morant Bay Rebellion (1865) 38, 51
Moravians 34-7, 94, 103
Muntu 17
Muslims 15, 55, 102-3
Myalism 23, 45-8, 109
Mysticism 49
Mythology 5-6, 20-2

Native Baptist Churches 35, 47, 49
Nativistic movements 85, 108-9
Negritude 91
Nigeria 14, 23, 30, 76
Nine-Day Wake 62-4
Nint-Night 63-4
Norris, Katrin 46
Ntikuma 22
Ntu 17
Nyame 19-20, 46
Nyankonpon 19-22, 46

Obayi 23
Obayifo 22-4, 40
Obeah 2, 23, 29, 40-3, 62, 100, 109
Ocho Rios 62

Index

Odum tree 44
Operation Friendship 95
Ophiolatry 23
Oracle 14
Orenda 17
Orisha 19-20

Panontism 6
Papua New Guinea 17, 31
Patterson, S. 55
Pentecostalism 48, 53, 92, 97-8, 100, 105, 111, 113
Pinnacle Affair 71-3
Plymouth Brethren 107
Pocomania 51-7, 61, 100, 109
Pokomo 55
Poltergeists 18
Portugal 9, 15, 25-6, 103
Possession 53-5, 60
Predials 10-11
Presbyterianism 35, 92, 111
Protestantism 30f
Punishment 29

Quakers 34, 109

Rain-making 65f
Rastafarians 68-91, 106, 109-11
Reformist type 109
Reincarnation 19
Revivalism 54-8, 61-2, 68, 92, 101
Revolutionary type 105-6
Rites de passage 46, 56, 58, 60, 100
Roman Catholicism 31-2, 82, 88, 92, 96, 111

Salvation Army 105
Saman 19-20, 43
Sasa 43
Schools 103
Seaga, Edward 61
Seventh-Day Adventism 92, 97, 100
Shadow-catching 44-8

Shango 19
Slave Rebellion 37
Slavery 10-6, 25-31
Society of Friends 34, 109
Somali 72
Sorcery 22-4, 29
Soul-washing 21-2, 54
Spanish slave code 25-31
Spiritualism 108-9
Sunsum 18

Tabaco 5
Tabu 20
Tacooma 44-5
Thaumaturgical type 54, 108-9
Totemism 21
Treaty of Madrid (1670) 10
Trickster figures 21-3, 45
Trinidad 26
Tuaregs 13, 15

Underhill, Dr 38
United Church of Jamaica 92-4
University of the West Indies 94
Utopian type 109-110

Venezuela 3, 59
Victorian Acts 42
Voodoo 23, 41, 53

Wakes 62-4
Weddings 66-7, 100
Wesleyan Missionary Society (1789) 35, 47
Whydah 16, 23, 41
Williams, J.J. 48
Wilson, B.R. 104, 109
Witchcraft 22-4, 29, 40-3

Yoruba 16-8

Zemes 6-8
Zionism 55-8, 61, 84, 88-9
Zombies 8, 60

You may also be interested in:
Christian Theology and African Traditions

by Matthew Michael

Christian theology is an increasingly non-Western enterprise now that the highest concentrations of Christians in the world are no longer found in the West. *Christian Theology and African Traditions* takes seriously the movement of Christianity from Western to non-Western settings and focuses on one place in particular: Africa. It repositions Christian theology and faith in order to engage the African traditions in the classical category of theology proper, as well as bibliology, anthropology, Christology, pneumatology, soteriology, ecclesiology, and eschatology. Matthew Michael provides unique insights into the problems that these classical and systematic categories pose to African Christianity, and offers a theological blueprint for non-Africans interested in knowing the nature and shape of Christian theology in non-Western settings.

Consequently, *Christian Theology and African Traditions* goes beyond the mere criticism of Western misrepresentation of African traditions to seeing how the Christian theology in its systematic character engages the African traditions. With this methodological template, the work describes in the space of twelve chapters the different classical teachings of the Christian faith on God, scriptures, spirits and demons, the nature of the human person, the persons of Christ, salvation, the Holy Spirit, the church, and the future life in dialogue with some specific traditions of the African people.

> 'Michael alternates between summarising historical approaches to a wide array of theological topics and exploring African traditions. ... Michael helpfully reminds us that there is much more to consider as we respond to God's love in our lives.'
> – **Revd Jesse Zink**, in *Church Times*

Matthew Michael is the Academic Dean of ECWA Theological Seminary, Kagoro, Nigeria. Dr. Michael has taught and presented papers on Christian theology in non-Western settings, issues in Old Testament, and African spirituality and world-views in universities and seminaries across Africa.

Published 2013

Paperback ISBN: 978 0 7188 9294 4
PDF ISBN: 978 0 7188 4152 2

You may also be interested in:
Meet Me at the Palaver
Narrative Pastoral Counselling in Postcolonial Contexts

by Tapiwa N. Mucherera

Meet Me at the Palaver shows the damaging impact of colonial Christianity on indigenous African communities. The book opens with stories of destructive change brought to indigenous contexts, where the culture, values, religion, and humanity of African peoples were often marginalised. Counselors in indigenous contexts need "to get off their couch or chair" and into the neighbourhoods, into those places made vulnerable to disease and poverty and by the collapse of "the palaver" and other traditional institutions of social stability.

Mucherera argues for a holistic narrative pastoral counseling approach to assess and service the three basic areas of human needs in indigenous African communities: body, mind, and spirit. The book presents a hopeful strategy of recovering stories, cultural traditions, and values that have been subjugated in the past as effective means for dealing with contemporary life in indigenous contexts such as Zimbabwe.

'A must read for all pastoral caregivers, pastors, counselors, and ministry students, since the narrative approach is an effective communication tool in today's cross cultural world.'
– **Anne Kiome Gatobu**, Asbury Theological Seminary

Tapiwa N. Mucherera is Professor of Pastoral Counseling at Asbury Theological Seminary and Assistant Provost in Florida. He is also the author of Pastoral Care from a Third World Perspective. The author is an ordained United Methodist pastor and has served in churches in Zimbabwe and in the United States.

Published 2010
Paperback ISBN: 978 0 7188 9219 7
PDF ISBN: 978 0 7188 4298 7